AN INTRODUCTION TO FAITH-BASED FINANCES

My MONEY Has a MISSION!

DR. LEE ANN B. MARINO, PH.D., D.MIN., D.D.

MY MONEY HAS A MISSION!

AN INSTRUCTIONAL GUIDE FOR FAITH-BASED FINANCES

DR. LEE ANN B. MARINO, PH.D., D.MIN., D.D.

Published by:
APOSTOLIC UNIVERSITY PRESS
(An imprint of The Righteous Pen Publications Group)
www.apostolicuniversity.org

Unless otherwise noted, all Scriptures are taken from the Holy Bible, **New Living Translation** copyright © 1996, 2004, 2007 by the Tyndale House Foundation. Used by permission of Tyndale House Publishers, Inc., Carol Stream, Illinois 60188. All rights reserved.

Scriptures marked KJV taken from the Authorized **King James Version of the Holy Bible**, Public Domain.

ISBN: 1-940197-41-4
13-Digit: 978-1-940197-41-8

Printed in the United States of America.

"AGAIN, THE KINGDOM OF HEAVEN CAN BE ILLUSTRATED BY THE STORY OF A MAN GOING ON A LONG TRIP. HE CALLED TOGETHER HIS SERVANTS AND ENTRUSTED HIS MONEY TO THEM WHILE HE WAS GONE. HE GAVE FIVE BAGS OF SILVER TO ONE, TWO BAGS OF SILVER TO ANOTHER, AND ONE BAG OF SILVER TO THE LAST—DIVIDING IT IN PROPORTION TO THEIR ABILITIES. HE THEN LEFT ON HIS TRIP.

"THE SERVANT WHO RECEIVED THE FIVE BAGS OF SILVER BEGAN TO INVEST THE MONEY AND EARNED FIVE MORE. THE SERVANT WITH TWO BAGS OF SILVER ALSO WENT TO WORK AND EARNED TWO MORE. BUT THE SERVANT WHO RECEIVED THE ONE BAG OF SILVER DUG A HOLE IN THE GROUND AND HID THE MASTER'S MONEY.

"AFTER A LONG TIME THEIR MASTER RETURNED FROM HIS TRIP AND CALLED THEM TO GIVE AN ACCOUNT OF HOW THEY HAD USED HIS MONEY. THE SERVANT TO WHOM HE HAD ENTRUSTED THE FIVE BAGS OF SILVER CAME FORWARD WITH FIVE MORE AND SAID, 'MASTER, YOU GAVE ME FIVE BAGS OF SILVER TO INVEST, AND I HAVE EARNED FIVE MORE.'

"THE MASTER WAS FULL OF PRAISE. 'WELL DONE, MY GOOD AND FAITHFUL SERVANT. YOU HAVE BEEN FAITHFUL IN HANDLING THIS SMALL AMOUNT, SO NOW I WILL GIVE YOU MANY MORE RESPONSIBILITIES. LET'S CELEBRATE TOGETHER!'

"THE SERVANT WHO HAD RECEIVED THE TWO BAGS OF SILVER CAME FORWARD AND SAID, 'MASTER, YOU GAVE ME TWO BAGS OF SILVER TO INVEST, AND I HAVE EARNED TWO MORE.'

"THE MASTER SAID, 'WELL DONE, MY GOOD AND FAITHFUL SERVANT. YOU HAVE BEEN FAITHFUL IN HANDLING THIS SMALL AMOUNT, SO NOW I WILL GIVE YOU MANY MORE RESPONSIBILITIES. LET'S CELEBRATE TOGETHER!'

"THEN THE SERVANT WITH THE ONE BAG OF SILVER CAME AND SAID, 'MASTER, I KNEW YOU WERE A HARSH MAN, HARVESTING CROPS YOU DIDN'T PLANT AND GATHERING CROPS YOU DIDN'T CULTIVATE. I WAS AFRAID I WOULD LOSE YOUR MONEY, SO I HID IT IN THE EARTH. LOOK, HERE IS YOUR MONEY BACK.'

"BUT THE MASTER REPLIED, 'YOU WICKED AND LAZY SERVANT! IF YOU KNEW I HARVESTED CROPS I DIDN'T PLANT AND GATHERED CROPS I DIDN'T CULTIVATE, WHY DIDN'T YOU DEPOSIT MY MONEY IN THE BANK? AT LEAST I COULD HAVE GOTTEN SOME INTEREST ON IT.'

"THEN HE ORDERED, 'TAKE THE MONEY FROM THIS SERVANT, AND GIVE IT TO THE ONE WITH THE TEN BAGS OF SILVER. TO THOSE WHO USE WELL WHAT THEY ARE GIVEN, EVEN MORE WILL BE GIVEN, AND THEY WILL HAVE AN ABUNDANCE. BUT FROM THOSE WHO DO NOTHING, EVEN WHAT LITTLE THEY HAVE WILL BE TAKEN AWAY. NOW THROW THIS USELESS SERVANT INTO OUTER DARKNESS, WHERE THERE WILL BE WEEPING AND GNASHING OF TEETH.'"

- MATTHEW 25:14-30

TABLE OF CONTENTS

ACKNOWLEDGEMENTS

I am most appreciative – and acknowledging – to all who are covered by Spitfire Apostolic Ministries and also those who are a part of Sanctuary International Fellowship Tabernacle – SIFT. Thanks to all of you, I have truly learned about the relevance of money in ministry.

1 WAITING FOR GOD TO DO IT

IT seems there was this man named Joe who found himself in dire trouble. His business had gone to bust and he was in serious financial trouble. He was so desperate that he decided to ask God for help.

He began to pray: "God, please help me. I've lost my business and if I don't get some money, I'm going to lose my house as well. Please let me win the lotto."

Lotto night came and somebody else won it. So Joe again prayed, "God, please let me win the lotto! I've lost my business, my house and I'm going to lose my car as well."

Lotto night came and Joe still had no luck. Once again, he prayed, "My God, why have You forsaken me? I've lost my business, my house, and my car. My wife and children are starving. I don't often ask You for help and I have always been a good servant to You. PLEASE just let me win the lotto this one time so I can get my life back in order."

Suddenly there was a blinding flash of light as the heavens opened and Joe was confronted by the voice of God Himself: "Joe, meet Me halfway on this. Buy a ticket."

We laugh at this story and find it humorous because there's part of us that wonders how Joe could ever have expected so much from God, especially in the face of reason. We sit back and say, "What was he thinking?" But there's a stark and rather bold reality in this story that many of us would probably rather overlook, and that's the part of us that feels just like Joe when it comes to our finances in relation to God. We hope that getting saved or more serious with God will erase our former financial indiscretions away, allowing us to pretend like they never happened. In this world that we live, God may forgive us, but the reality is the banks, credit card debtors, hospitals, doctors, and others we owe money to aren't quite so understanding. It doesn't help that we often turn on the television to hear out-of-balance teaching on finances from preachers themselves, who tell us that how much money we have is a sign of our faith. Some go as far as to promise they can get us out of debt by praying over pictures or dollar amounts if we are willing to send them large amounts of money. All of this sounds appealing, especially in a world where we don't want to take responsibility for having been so irresponsible with money. We'd rather the problems go away instead of having to face the idea that we might have to "meet God halfway."

When it comes to our money, we have to face facts that we must be both responsible with our expenses and responsible with how we use our money, because as a whole, the way the church approaches money is harmful to both the well-being of its members and of its operations, in and of itself. I have watched people plunge into financial ruin, both good ministers and good Christians, because they didn't understand the relationship they had with their money. I have watched too many believers lose their houses, their property, and in a certain sense, their minds as they lived completely out of touch with what they had. I've seen believers who believed in prosperity fall as well as those who felt that God expected His people to make do with what they had, and the end result was the same. It was the same because on both sides of very extreme thinking, people lack the balance needed to take the Word of God in perspective and understand the relationship they need to have with money and all it truly signifies in the life of the believer.

I am not, by any stretch of the imagination, a financial adviser. If you want complicated advice about a specific financial situation, you will need to consult with a qualified professional about your matters at hand. If you are looking for specified financial advice, I can't give it to you. What I know about stocks and bonds probably couldn't even fill one of these pages. I have spent years trying to dissect and navigate the world of ministry under incredibly dire circumstances, especially with limited resources. I have even made financial mistakes myself, as much as I do try to make better financial decisions. I deal with rent, bills, payments, loans, credit history, and everything else that normal people deal with. I might not always have the technical answers of an accountant, but after twenty years of dealing with personal, business, and ministry finances, I have learned a thing or two about money, and about how to best allot spending.

Proverbs 10:16: *THE EARNINGS OF THE GODLY ENHANCE THEIR LIVES, BUT EVIL PEOPLE SQUANDER THEIR MONEY ON SIN.*

Even though I might not be an accountant, I do know the Word of God, and the fact that His Word brings us to life in every area of our circumstances. We talk a lot about playing by God's rules and applying God's Word, but I don't think we understand how to do that in many areas of our lives, specifically when it comes to money. We see and hear so many extremes about what God wants for us, we aren't able to sit back and truly develop a needed understanding of money, how money works, and how we should work our money. Yes, living within God's will does mean we partner with Him for a sense of financial success, but just how that manifests depends largely on how we understand it and interpret success and purpose with our money.

When we are born again, we undergo redemption from sin; however, that does not mean that all the consequences from the sin we have repented from magically disappear. We still often have to make decisions to clean up our existing circumstances, and our finances are no different. Just as before being saved we lived only for ourselves, so do we spend only for ourselves. Just because we have prayed the Sinner's Prayer, asked Jesus into our lives, been baptized, speak in tongues, or experienced profound conversion on a certain level does not mean that we stop having problems or that we don't have to discipline ourselves for success. Salvation is a choice, and making that one choice means we must therefore make saved choices because our salvation gives us the power to do just that. We have to trade in unforgiveness for forgiveness, evil for life, and yes, even bad financial choices for good ones so our Kingdom power can be visible to all.

Your money has a mission! As hard as it might be to believe, your money is destined to be put to good use because you are a believer. Everything in our lives should reflect the saving transformation that God has done within us: our character, our habits, our obedience, our relationships, our usage of time, and yes, even our finances and financial choices. Many ask for prayer for their finances, but some of what this comes down to is changing the way you view money and the relationship you have with it. If your finances aren't saved, it's time to learn how they can be! You can make saved choices when it comes to your finances and clean up even the worst financial situation with God's help. I make the joke that sometimes despite our best efforts, we are called to baptize our checkbooks, baptize our bank accounts, baptize our circumstances, and most of all, baptize our minds so that our attitudes as pertain to money can change and we can start adopting new principles about money.

JOURNALING

- Get yourself a journal specifically for this project.

2 MONEY, MONEY, MONEY...MON-EY!

To be honest, I don't like writing about money. I'd much rather write about faith, or do a Bible book commentary on one of the prophets, or...just about anything besides talking about money. I think it doesn't interest me because I hear so much about it, all the time. Whether in church, flipping through the channels on television, or even having to go over it personally, I get bored of hearing about, talking about, and especially thinking about...money. It becomes a gigantic yawn, something we've gone over, time and time again, that doesn't get more fascinating with time. Numbers are numbers and money comes down to numbers, and numbers remind me too much of that math class I thought I'd never pass...

Or does it?

As bored as I might be with hearing about money and might not to write about it, the truth is that we don't hear the truth about money in most of the circles we follow. We hear things about money or talk of it, but we really don't hear what we need to so our relationship with money can change. The way we approach money, especially within church, is hurting ALL of us. It is causing us all to be broke, to be stressed, to be frustrated, and to always be looking for something to come down the pike, that magical, financial miracle to change our world around. When it doesn't come, week after week, month after month, year after year, we have to step back and assess our financial situations to see what we can do differently to change our situations.

So this chapter is a money boot camp, of sorts: what it is, what we do, how it works, and some basics that, as we go along in this book, will help give us the foundations to financial empowerment.

WHAT IS MONEY?

It's hard to define money, because in many ways, money isn't just a "thing." Money is also a concept with many representations in this life. In its literal sense, money is currency, found in paper, digitalized, or coin format, that is used as part of an exchange for goods or services. It is almost always created by a government for use in this exchange by its citizens. Beyond this literal definition of what money is, money is hard to define. It is something that defines the way people live the world over, and the comforts and conveniences they may (or may not) have as a result. In terms of history, money began with bartering systems, trade and interaction between people for services and goods, and exists down to the current day and age.

WHAT ARE FINANCES?

Most of us already know finances relate to money, but some might be unsure of how finances relate to money and just what they are. The term "finances" is used in relation to money, but they are more than money. They are the entire amount of our assets and how we spend those assets. It is about acquiring money, budgeting, spending, and then re-earning – and starting the entire cycle all over again. Finances are both our wealth input and output, not just a dollar amount of how much we have. Finances recognize that what we use is as relevant as what we earn and have, and that we must take both in account in considering the condition of our monetary state. Your financial budget is the record of how your spend your money weekly, monthly, or yearly. It shows how the bulk of money is spent. Considering both, budgeting and finances, are a summary of your financial account.

Ecclesiastes 10:19: *A FEAST IS MADE FOR LAUGHTER, AND WINE MAKETH MERRY: BUT MONEY ANSWERETH ALL THINGS.* (KJV)

We tend to think that finances only pertain to one aspect of our lives, but truthfully, they apply to all areas of our lives. They might be one specific thing, but they extend into many different areas of our living. Think of this concept in terms of marriage. One wouldn't say that marriage only applies to one part of your life. If that were true, marital troubles wouldn't affect children, friendships, and yes, marital finances. The parallel is the same here. Even though finances represent one part of our lives, they don't just affect a singular aspect of your life. Don't get the mistaken idea that financial irresponsibility can't affect other aspects of your life, which this errored thinking perpetuates. How we operate our finances shows forth how we live in other areas of our lives, and if we are financially problematic, odds are good that we are problematic elsewhere, as well. The same is true for having good finances and making good financial decisions. Doing so will make things better in our lives, overall, in many ways.

WHY BE SERIOUS ABOUT FINANCES?

Financial disciplines are often taught to be something that should come with age. Most people expect that once an individual moves out and lives on their own, having a job and maintaining expenses such as a home or apartment and a car, they should have a handle on their financial matters. The problem with this logic is that financial discipline is not something ever taught in school, and it is also not something that they see within the media as they grow up. What they see in their favorite celebrities and artists is financial opulence, spending extravagant amounts of money on things that other people either do not have access to or are unable to spend so much of their income to purchase or do. With the increases in "reality TV" pushing these lifestyles as normal or as things that are "reality," more people are spending money on technology, designer items, lavish trips and houses...and getting themselves in debt for it, every step of the way.

The church is no exception to this world of increasing opulence. Discussion about helping the poor or rebuilding our inner-city neighborhoods has been replaced with encouragement to give money to big-name preachers because God "will do the same for you" if you give enough to them. Where people used to talk about being missionaries or spreading the Gospel, now people go into ministry thinking it will lead them into the spotlight of a mega-church or mega-ministry. The more we talk about money, the more obvious it is that we have no idea at all what we are talking about. Preaching about such encourages believers to aspire for the same lifestyles and living that we see on television that, is in reality, only accessible to a very small percentage of the population. I've watched more than one person chase after that dream to the detriment of their families, their own physical health and well-being, their spirituality, and yes, even their sense of reality.

There is one thing that the big preachers who are always talking about money are right about: God does care about our finances, and He does care about what we do with our money. God expects us to be serious about financial matters because how we handle our financial matters affects our entire lives. Everything about us should serve as a witness once we are saved, and that includes how we handle our money. Beyond witness, which most likely is probably an obvious facet, I don't believe it is God's will for His people to be so far in debt that they are unable to pay it off or that they feel they need to compete with others through financial spending. Spending one's life bound and controlled by money is a pretty uncomfortable and awful way to live, and if God calls us to have an abundant life, that means we can't have it if we are always paying out or spending too much.

The problem with living this kind of lifestyle is that far too few are hearing the truth about God and His approach to finances before they get themselves into serious financial trouble. Even if someone can afford to live more over the top than the average person, living that lifestyle gets old, quickly. Too often in life people only get serious about financial matters when there is something they seek to do or further in their lives, or when they run into roadblocks because they have mismanaged their money. By that time, they are usually in some kind of financial mess already difficult to repair. This is why God wants us to always be serious in financial matters: He always has something He wants to do through us for both ourselves and the greater good of God's Kingdom. Our money has more of a mission than to sit in a bank account or be frittered away on frivolous pursuits.

Haggai 2:8: *THE SILVER IS MINE, AND THE GOLD IS MINE, SAYS THE LORD OF HEAVEN'S ARMIES.*

I've heard this verse slanted many different ways over the years, and I will talk a little more about it in a later chapter. I want us to look at it here, though, because God has every reason to be interested in our finances and to take interest in them. This verse alone proves that the concept of our wealth and our money resources originally came from the ground, the very earth that God created. This passage is a point of origins claim. We think what we have is ours, but it's not. Everything we have is from God, including any finances we have received, and that means out of the generous bounty we have received from Him, we must give back to Him. When we honor God with our finances, including Him as a part of our financial responsibility, He blesses us that in turn we may bless Him and others. It is a wonderful cycle that is much better than the cycle of financial burden, in which we in turn acquire debt and loss, until something "more important" comes along that suddenly makes us realize what we've done in terms of making a mess out of our money.

Financial responsibility means setting priorities. It means we do not spend money we do not have on frivolous things we do not need when we cannot afford to do so, and that we do not spend amounts of money that we don't have. We gain perspective that while it is perfectly all right to do something nice and even have nice things, it's not a drive or a need that we feel like we must pursue in order to "be somebody." It means not misusing credit or debit cards, not bouncing checks, and being sure things like rent and mortgage payments are paid before social activities are entertained. It means we pay our taxes and other financial responsibilities to state and country. Most relevant and important, before all other things, we give the first part of our finances to God in the form of a tithe and we support the work of God with offerings to the Kingdom.

We shall discuss all of this in this book, in one form or another. Right now, as we go into the details of this book, I ask you to think to yourself: how do you feel about money? This question is important, especially as we go through the rest of this chapter.

YOUR RELATIONSHIP WITH MONEY

All of us have a relationship with the almighty dollar, even if we think we don't. If you don't have a dime to your name, you still have a relationship with money. Your relationship with money is, most likely complicated, and is related to many of the different things we will speak on in this chapter. While I am a big advocate of the belief that we don't need to understand why we do everything we do in order to make a change in our lives, I do think that recognizing patterns of behavior with money help us to make – and maintain – the changes needed to walk in financial victory.

Psalm 112:5: *GIVE ME AN EAGERNESS FOR YOUR LAWS RATHER THAN A LOVE FOR MONEY!*

How do you feel about money? Do you love it? Do you have it? Do you wish you had more of it? What do you associate with money? Most likely, you have a certain awareness of the necessity of money in your life, and truth be told, that awareness probably dominates a lot of your thought process. You get concerned when you are uncertain about where the needed funds will come from. You are upset when you don't have the money to do something or fund something that you want to do. You might be jealous, envious, or angry over the financial status that someone else seems to have, especially if they don't seem to be doing anything to maintain it or haven't done anything to earn it within your mind's eye view. You might want to do so much more, but feel so bound by your financial situations.

I don't mean to imply, nor suggest, that we live in a world where we are adequately compensated for the work that we do or that things are of great expense in today's society. I am the first one online explaining to foreign ministers how high the cost of living is in the western world, and that the way western society is constructed means we have more – and higher – expenses that we would deem as "necessities" than they do in other countries. At the same time, the vicious cycle that keeps causing our expenses to go up is the commodity, luxury-based world that we live in that we are willing to pay for, time and time again. An increasing amount of money in the western world is spent on entertainment or recreational venues, which has caused things that used to be regarded as professions – whether professional writing (authors), music production, professional food and beverage sales, sporting events, and beyond – are all now considered hobbies and luxuries, things that we should charge the individuals who desire to pursue them for rather than making money on the other side. This is genius, in a certain sense, because it has now created a market where those who desire to pursue these venues have to pay, time and time again, for the services. Then when people buy the product, money is usually made off the purchasers as well as those who receive the service. Those who are lucky enough to break into the market often then become heroes to those who have not, which means that those who don't make it then spend their money lining the pockets of those who have in an attempt to figure out what is so great about them.

The way we spend money today is radically different than it was fifty, twenty, even ten years ago. When I was growing up, spending money was something reserved for the rich, and those who didn't have a lot of money did without things. In those days, things seemed expensive, but by modern standards, they don't seem that unreasonable. Nowadays, medical and educational costs are out of control, even when people have planned through insurance and spending. Most college graduates start their adult lives in debt before they even have a job. Coupled with more and more spending when it comes to entertainment venues or trying to pursue different aspects of life, you have a royal financial mess, a dysfunctional relationship with money, caused in large part by always thinking that the answers to every financial problem is more money.

The answer to financial problems isn't more money; it is better spending habits, and money spent in different ways. Those come about as we stop seeing money as the answer to all our problems and start reassessing need, versus want. In order to do this, let's look at where we got some of our ideas about money in the first place.

FAMILY AND MONEY

How we handle money is largely taught, and were learned, perhaps, without a specific word or financial lesson. Your first encounters with money were, most likely, those you encountered in your household. Whether you grew up around money or not, you probably picked up on certain things about finances just from being around your family. For example, someone was probably angry at someone at some point in time because of a loan or borrowed money that was never returned. If you received an allowance, you learned that working hard at something was a good way to get money to do the things you wanted to do. Your parents or guardians probably fought about money at some point in time, whether it was money that was spent without the other partner knowing or money that was needed for something and wasn't there. Maybe one of your parents was a free-spender, while your other parent or guardian was worried about cleaning up after their irresponsibility. Maybe someone lost their job or lost a business. Maybe your family was in debt and tried not to look like they were, or maybe they tried to avoid debt. If you were indulged with expensive gifts or items at a young age, you probably learned quickly that money was dispensable, and trusted your family would keep making and providing money, no matter what you did with what was given to you.

You watched your family live as generous givers, takers, providers, sharers, or maybe even stealers, and you watched the way they either explained or justified (sometimes without a word) their behavior.

These complicated life situations show just how intricate money often is, in unspoken and subtle ways, throughout our lives. While people were living their lives and trying to provide in ways they knew how, their approaches to money weren't things that blew in and then blew out of life. How your family approached money and their honesty when it came to money affects you, too, maybe even right down to this present day. It affects how you see money and feel about it, and the way you perceive your own values when it comes to giving. You either mimic what they did or want to do the exact opposite, which can be just as bad.

SELF-ESTEEM AND MONEY

I don't think it's a big secret that a great amount of who we are as people is societally tied up in how much money we have or how much money others think we have. We learn it as kids: the one who has the most toys, the best shoes, the most up-to-date electronics is the one who "wins." The kid at school who had the most materially was the kid everyone wanted to be around, everyone wanted to imitate, and everyone wanted to be seen with. They might have even gotten special treatment from teachers or other authority figures, allowed to slide by with things that other children would have been punished for.

Into our teen years and now as adults, a certain sense of shame often accompanies not having the income or things that others have. We learned this because of how we were treated when someone had more, and we had less, as was seen in the example above. Maybe we were teased for having hand-me-down clothing or we were mocked for not having the latest gadgets or toys. Whatever experience we had, we learned that having less was something to be shamed, and having more was better. This contradicted every message we would hear about money socially (which we will talk about next), but it was the message burned in our brains: if we can have more of this forbidden money thing, we can have a better life. People will like us and respect us, and if we don't have money, we should feel bad about ourselves.

Now that we are grown, this intimate, confusing message about money has translated to say much about our own self-perception and self-esteem. We get easily depressed and discouraged if we don't have the money we want to do something and we expect other people to make us feel better when we experience financial lack. When we find ourselves unable to function, we want an excuse to...you guessed it...spend money. We tell ourselves that we "deserve" whatever it is, be some sort of night out, treat, or something that we simply can't afford. It sounds odd when we make it plain, but we handle our depression over not having enough money by spending money we don't have.

1 Timothy 6:17: *TEACH THOSE WHO ARE RICH IN THIS WORLD NOT TO BE PROUD AND NOT TO TRUST IN THEIR MONEY, WHICH IS SO UNRELIABLE. THEIR TRUST SHOULD BE IN GOD, WHO RICHLY GIVES US ALL WE NEED FOR OUR ENJOYMENT.*

If we didn't so intimately tie our self-worth with our finances, we would handle our money differently. The money spent on elective plastic surgery would dry up quickly. The endless search for fortune and fame lost in pyramid schemes and weight loss drugs would end. We wouldn't buy half the products we try to buy to look thinner, younger, richer, more powerful, or more dominant in the social scene. We wouldn't be so tempted to overspend and we would probably be more generous in our giving to others. That same critical, judgmental eye that put us down unless we were super-rich we now use on others, always wondering why have less than we do and assuming there is something they could do to get out of it if they tried hard enough. Using money to get up and down the social ladder would end. It's that simple, and that complicated.

IS MONEY THE ROOT OF ALL EVIL?

I still remember the old Pink Floyd video for the song, *Money*. The first line of that song is probably what has stuck with me the most: "Money...so they say...is the root of all evil today." Interesting as the video was with many different images of different financial forms and amounts, Pink Floyd got one thing wrong. There is nothing anywhere in the

Bible that states money itself is the root of all evil. Yet even though there is nothing that states that money itself is evil, there are plenty of people (Pink Floyd included) who spread the rumor around that money itself is evil, and having it is wrong, trying to utilize it is bad, and that money is a petty, dirty thing to be avoided.

Yet…despite these messages…none of us are stupid. We all know that having money entitles certain privileges, certain concepts, and certain ideals. If we look at the life of a monk or nun in poverty and then look at the life of the rich and famous, it doesn't take long until we figure out which one we want more. This stuff that we've heard is absolutely no good all our lives is suddenly the very thing we want…which makes it forbidden.

Forbidden is never good. Forbidden gets us into trouble, every time. Why? Forbidden throws us right into the love of something taboo, and when we get in that place with money, we get into a danger zone. The extremes we've heard about money over our lifetimes has made money a foreign, exotic, unobtainable thing that we yearn after and desire in the same way that anything else seen as taboo is often viewed. It's no wonder, then, that many people fall into the trap of the love of money, which the Bible does clarify is a problem. It might not ever say that money itself is evil, but the love of money is spoken of in the Bible as the root of all evil.

Proverbs 1:19: *SUCH IS THE FATE OF ALL WHO ARE GREEDY FOR MONEY; IT ROBS THEM OF LIFE.*

Ecclesiastes 5:10: *THOSE WHO LOVE MONEY WILL NEVER HAVE ENOUGH. HOW MEANINGLESS TO THINK THAT WEALTH BRINGS TRUE HAPPINESS!*

1 Timothy 6:10: *FOR THE LOVE OF MONEY IS THE ROOT OF ALL KINDS OF EVIL. AND SOME PEOPLE, CRAVING MONEY, HAVE WANDERED FROM THE TRUE FAITH AND PIERCED THEMSELVES WITH MANY SORROWS.*

If you look around our world, there is no way to deny that it's true: the love of money is the root of all evil. When people pursue money, idolize it, and love it above anything else in their lives, they are willing to do anything to get it. They will beg, borrow, steal, enslave, abuse, mistreat, and lie in order to get the money they crave in their lives. As a result, the love of money takes people down a long and winding road that leads to serious destruction and problems.

Yes, we know the love of money is a problem. More than that, there are many who are displaying the principle that money also reveals what we love and what is most important to us. There are more people who love what money represents than money itself, and they love and covet the idea of having more or having the most and what it will do for them. Where, what, and how we spend our money says a lot about us as people, and many times, we are saying that we love things with our mouths, but our finances bespeak something to the contrary. While yes, the love of money is certainly a problem, it is also a problem if we are mishandling or money or if we are misusing it in some way for the wrong purposes because our hearts, minds, and love are in the wrong things or in things the wrong way.

Loving money is evil. Idolizing money is evil. How people sometimes use money is evil. Money, in and of itself, is not evil. Worshiping the ideology that money often creates, however, is evil.

WORSHIPING THE IDEOLOGY OF MONEY

I am including this section here because the truth about most people is that they do worship money, but they worship it in a sense by which it is distanced from money itself, thus leading people to think that they aren't really worshipping money. The truth is they might not be worshipping money itself, but they are worshipping the ideal that money creates, and the concept of what money can do. This is far more common than you might think, and often lurks in lives in ways that we don't consider.

If you carefully study the media and media images, very, very few of the people who immerge today as popular artists are what we would have classified as "talented" in prior decades. Very few of them write their own lyrics, very few of them can sing, act, or dance naturally, without the assistance of enhancing digital media, and the majority of them all look alike, in some way, shape, or form. In fact, if you listen to them on the radio or look at them online, it's very possible you have trouble telling many of them apart. This isn't an accident, and it's not as simple as all the people who look alike are the people who are selected to be talented.

The truth is that the entertainment industries aren't just randomly selecting people based on talents or abilities. We've already established a lot of them aren't really that extraordinary, at least no more extraordinary than the kid in the neighborhood with a talent. What places someone in entertainment today is their ability to morph or transform into an image that the media knows it can sell to an eager – and willing to pay – public. It's about finding someone that the media can turn into the "ideal" person or image that others are willing to pay to see and endorse, morphing them into that persona.

This process is known as branding, or selling an image. Branding has long been associated with commercial products, and now with the emergence of celebrities, individuals now brand themselves in order to make money by selling concerts, promotional items, movies, and their very personal – self – images. These images are morphed into a commercially acceptable image, one that will sell whatever medium is used to make that image sell and grow in popularity so that individual's image will reap a financial profit.

If you have patronized a band's music concert, stood in line for Nike sneakers, scoured the internet for Kardashian cosmetics, gone without food or rent to go and see a show, camped out to purchase *Star Wars* tickets, bought a tabloid magazine, or bought tickets to see a popular preacher who sold out your local auditorium, you have participated in the system of branding. You see whoever that artist, actor, celebrity, preacher, or other person in the light of whatever it is that they are selling, and you have been willing to pay for it.

The catch with branding is that the brand someone is selling – that you are all-too-willing to pay for – is most likely not even that person. It's a persona that was created by marketing directors, advertising campaigns, and people who can tell others what sells or doesn't sell. It doesn't mean the people agree with or believe in what they say, sing, use, or do, or that they have any connection to that persona, whatsoever. They are a created image, something there to sell a product, to make money. That means whenever we make sure we are first in line, in the first row, first one to buy tickets, first one to see the movie, first one to get the album, and the biggest product of the fan club, we are participating in the creation of that persona to make money.

Psalm 106:36: *THEY WORSHIPED THEIR IDOLS, WHICH LED TO THEIR DOWNFALL.*

Ezekiel 7:20: *THEY WERE PROUD OF THEIR BEAUTIFUL JEWELRY AND USED IT TO MAKE DETESTABLE IDOLS AND VILE IMAGES. THEREFORE, I WILL MAKE ALL THEIR WEALTH DISGUSTING TO THEM.*

Ezekiel 14:5: *I WILL DO THIS TO CAPTURE THE MINDS AND HEARTS OF ALL MY PEOPLE WHO HAVE TURNED FROM ME TO WORSHIP THEIR DETESTABLE IDOLS.*

Romans 1:23: *AND INSTEAD OF WORSHIPING THE GLORIOUS, EVER-LIVING GOD, THEY WORSHIPED IDOLS*

MADE TO LOOK LIKE MERE PEOPLE AND BIRDS AND ANIMALS AND REPTILES.

It isn't a secret that people in society tend to idolize and worship those whose image they like. I have met many people who will willingly forsake values, ideals, concepts, and even good sense to follow after a preacher, a singer, an actor, an artist, or some other media celebrity figure in order to conform into the image of what they have. If we are doing this on any level – it's idolatry, and it is a form of supporting the love of money. We are making sure that someone else can chase after and afford that opulence at our own expense, and promote that image to others. I am not saying it's wrong to like what someone does or has to say who is famous, but there is something wrong with it when we are willing to give up so much of our lives, our identities, and yes, even our finances for it. There is something wrong with the fact that too many times, we are chasing a persona and thinking it embodies something we need to have or support to the neglect of our own lives, ideals and thoughts, and that we encourage others to do the same in many different ways. It's the love of money, but it is the love of money in a different way: it is enabling the love of money by people who are willing to compromise themselves to get it, and it is loving what that lifestyle represents to those who do not have it.

MONEY AND WANTING TO BELONG

We use the expression, "Keeping up with the Joneses" to refer to the social pressure to have what those around you also have. For example, if the neighbors have a four-door car and you have a two-door car, the expectation is to go and get a bigger four-door car to make sure that the neighbors don't outdo what you have. It is a root of competition, something that says we have to be the biggest and best, and we're going to use money to outdo everyone around us.

Amos 3:10: *"MY PEOPLE HAVE FORGOTTEN HOW TO DO RIGHT," SAYS THE LORD. "THEIR FORTRESSES ARE FILLED WITH WEALTH TAKEN BY THEFT AND VIOLENCE."*

1 Timothy 6:6: *YET TRUE GODLINESS WITH CONTENTMENT IS ITSELF GREAT WEALTH.*

Keeping up with the Joneses is probably one of the worst messages we've gotten as a society, and certainly one of the most destructive. It re-echoes the message we got as kids that what dictates our social status is our income and that we should be willing to shell out money to fit into a grander scheme of things. There's a bigger catch behind this, however, and it relates to branding, as we spoke of earlier. The secret of every advertising campaign and every celebrity or social branding is the concept of personal endorsement. Whenever we engage in advertising as consumers, we are being told that we should see ourselves in the image of whatever we are being sold. It means that whenever you buy into the advertising for a product, you are buying a lot more than just that product; you are also buying a message about yourself, about your neighbors, about fitting into society, about being better than someone else, and about who that advertiser believes you think you should become.

If this sounds problematic, it gets worse. Advertisers hit home at insecurities, emotions, feelings, thoughts, and concepts that we have about competing with other people. Whether it's because we feel inferior or we just want to gain a status to be on top, advertising's chief measure is how we look or feel about ourselves and what we have versus what someone else might have or feel. That advertising edge keeps us spending money left and right on things that are often overpriced, such as vacations at the peak time of the year, electronic devices the second they come out, designer clothes that come from the same factory in China as the clothes that are made by off-brands, brand-new automobiles, homes we cannot afford, and lifestyles that involve expenses we don't need to incur.

CHRISTIANS AND SOCIAL PRESSURES

I would tell you that Christianity has always embraced the idea of being counter-culture, but the truth is that throughout most of its history, Christianity has often blended in with the rest of society, looking the same and chasing many of the same pursuits. Our modern church is no different, except with one glaring exception: Now Christians claim to be different, all the while doing the same things and engaging in the same branding and marketing techniques used to make celebrities famous. Whether it's an all-pink gift bag for Mother's Day or forest-green pocket knives with Bible verses that encourage "male" values, Christians who run out to see what are deemed "Christian-themed" movies, buy "Christian-themed" T-shirts, or support "Christian-deemed" causes, Christians are also wildly lining the pockets of clever merchandisers who sell America's favorite preachers, ideals, and feed fear factors left, right, and sideways. Instead of being different, I meet too many Christians who as consumer-minded and falling for the same branding techniques with different items. Whether the T-shirt has a band on it or a Bible verse, you're still overpaying for a T-shirt because you want whatever is printed on it.

1 Timothy 6:3-5: *SOME PEOPLE MAY CONTRADICT OUR TEACHING, BUT THESE ARE THE WHOLESOME TEACHINGS OF THE LORD JESUS CHRIST. THESE TEACHINGS PROMOTE A GODLY LIFE. ANYONE WHO TEACHES SOMETHING DIFFERENT IS ARROGANT AND LACKS UNDERSTANDING. SUCH A PERSON HAS AN UNHEALTHY DESIRE TO QUIBBLE OVER THE MEANING OF WORDS. THIS STIRS UP ARGUMENTS ENDING IN JEALOUSY, DIVISION, SLANDER, AND EVIL SUSPICIONS. THESE PEOPLE ALWAYS CAUSE TROUBLE. THEIR MINDS ARE CORRUPT, AND THEY HAVE TURNED THEIR BACKS ON THE TRUTH. TO THEM, A SHOW OF GODLINESS IS JUST A WAY TO BECOME WEALTHY.*

When we consider that there are denominations that have spent their entire histories trying to avoid commercialism in any form, it is ironic to note the extremes we see in many other churches. The extremes that we see in Christian spending often vary, including extremes in expensive women's and men's attire or the drive to resemble a rock concert and wear the latest in designer fashions for youth, money spent on Christian music downloads or concerts, gear, accessories, or even Bibles and books, Christians crossing most denominations spend a great amount of money on fashionable Christian trends that relate to different fads and winds of doctrine that trail through the church every few years.

SPIRITUALITY BEHIND COMMERCIALISM

If we understand the spiritual realm, we know that there are usually spiritual factors behind natural or worldly things we encounter in this world. Truth be told, we are paying an extremely high price for the different issues we have discussed in this chapter. Starting out when we are young, we get certain ideas in our heads about money, having money, and pursuing money. We pursue the love of money without even knowing it and support the love of money as we chase after branding and different fads. Even though we have become Christians, we often chase after trends as much as we did before becoming saved, just in new ways (and sometimes they are even the same fads!). We associate money with status, power, wanting to belong, wanting to be a part of something bigger than ourselves...and we are drowning in debt and doctrines that encourage us to keep pursuing these things, even though they are unreasonable and we can't afford them. Beyond this, our disordered relationship and attitudes as pertain to money are a sign of something deeper, of identity problems rooted in worldly competition and self-depreciation in the name of being a personal concept that is unrealistic and doesn't exist.

Then we go into God's house and skimp on our Kingdom giving because we have overspent in other areas of our lives, chasing after identities and concepts that are not and should not be who we are anymore. We expect God and our spiritual leaders to understand, and we hope that they will be able to "make do" with what we feel we are able to give. We justify not tithing because we won't be able to afford something else that helps give us social status if we do it, and we never give above or beyond what we think we can give. We pray that God will send someone who is more financially capable to help out our leaders, someone who can meet all their needs, because we measure up our meager amount of giving against the need and know that we can't financially offer it on our own. Sure, we might have money for the preacher on television or to buy tickets to a major Christian event, but we see that as acceptable – and somehow different – when it's time to make an offering to the church or ministry we formally sit under.

Hebrews 13:5: *DON'T LOVE MONEY; BE SATISFIED WITH WHAT YOU HAVE. FOR GOD HAS SAID, "I WILL NEVER FAIL YOU. I WILL NEVER ABANDON YOU."*

If you are a believer, I do hope that hearing this scenario out loud sounds as errored and problematic as it is. Truth be told, the majority of believers think this way, and this thinking is killing ministries before they even have a chance to go anywhere. It's obvious that, for the average Christian, the pursuit to be someone through money, to be someone greater than their neighbors, and to bury all their insecurities with assorted products trumps the need and desire to be a part of the Kingdom of God and participate in it fully, finances included.

If we are truly in Christ, our thinking about everything – including our relationship with money and our concepts about finances – should change. If it hasn't, we need to start to take the steps to bring about that change and look over our financial perspectives as an area of our lives in need of healing and reform as much as any other aspect of our lives. Until we do this, we will continue to chase emotional rainbows through money and live with more deficits than improvements. If we believe in victory, then we should seek it here, too.

JOURNALING

- Write about what you believe money can get you in your life.
- Write about a story from your life that involved a lesson about the differences

between rich and poor. How did this incident effect your ideas about money?
- What social pressures have you felt to spend money as a Christian?

3 WHERE YOUR TREASURE IS...

WE'VE all heard the Bible verse, *Wherever your treasure is, the desires of your heart will also be.* (Matthew 6:21) We've used it all sorts of ways: to indicate what our gifts are, to talk about what is important to us, even to stir us to a bigger offering in the church. All of these approaches to treasures and our hearts is fascinating, even interesting...but are they accurate?

The truth with the Scriptures and money is the way we tend to take things out of context and we tend to miss the things we don't want to hear and scream louder the things that might not be in there, at all. As we do with most things we don't like or don't want to deal with the truth about, we eschew the Biblical principles and attitudes about money so that we can avoid dealing with reality. In our attempts to avoid reality, we keep getting farther…and farther…and farther out of touch with the truth.

The Bible tells us outright that it is the truth that will set us free, not a lie. That means all these lies we keep running around and believing, all the while blaming them on Scripture, aren't going to set us free. What will set us free is breaking through our denial, stop avoiding the difficult questions about money and about financial matters, and start addressing them with the truth so we can walk in our financial victories.

…THERE YOUR HEART IS, ALSO

The verse I opened this chapter with is Matthew 6:21. We are going to back up to verse 19 and look at verses 19-21, in order to help the verse, itself, make sense.

Matthew 6:19-21: *DON'T STORE UP TREASURES HERE ON EARTH, WHERE MOTHS EAT THEM AND RUST DESTROYS THEM, AND WHERE THIEVES BREAK IN AND STEAL. STORE YOUR TREASURES IN HEAVEN, WHERE MOTHS AND RUST CANNOT DESTROY, AND THIEVES DO NOT BREAK IN AND STEAL. WHEREVER YOUR TREASURE IS, THERE THE DESIRES OF YOUR HEART WILL ALSO BE.*

Looking at the surrounding verses clarifies the passage is speaking about money in all its forms: how we spend it, why we spend it, and what we save our money for. In terms of the specific verse, verse 21, there are two parts to its thoughts. The first is where your treasure is, and the second is there your heart will be, also. If we are going to get real as to what this passage means, we need to break up the verse and look at each part separately, and then put it together.

- **Where your treasure is** – I am not going to get real deep or esoteric with this verse, to talk about it in terms of all the depths and treasures we have within us as spiritual gifts. I suppose that can apply in a certain sense, but if we look at verses 19 and 20, it does clarify the verse is not talking about anything that super deep. This passage is about money, plain and simple. The Bible is telling us about financial matters and clarifying that earthly hoarding, storing up for earthly benefit, and to amass things for no other reason than to be rich is not Kingdom, nor is it godly. The passage is telling us that where our treasure is – if we are holding our resources for earthly things – they will remain for earthly aspirations. The question is, where does your aspiration lie?

- **There your heart will be, also** – Your heart can't be on earth and in heaven at the same time. We can't be earthly minded and spiritually minded at the same time. If we want the things of this world, they come at the price of eternal things. Thus, wherever your treasure is – if it's in things, if it's in earthly matters, if it's in the world – then there your heart is, not on the things we often might claim.

This means that an awful lot of Christians are lying about their priorities. The Bible is clear here, plain as day: we can't ride the fence when it comes to things that pertain to money, because money reveals our hearts. Where our hearts lie is where our money is not only spent, but what it is saved up for, what we are eager to spend our money on, how we store it, what we store it for, how it is spent, and how it is used. In other words: Money is a revealer of what is most important to us in our lives, what we want to accomplish, what we want to do, where we are going, and where the deepest part of us lies.

So let's get it straight up: You can tell me (or any other minister, for that matter) all day long about how God is first in your life, how you want to be in ministry, how your priorities are the things of God, how you want to do more for the Kingdom, but how you handle your money is going to be the deciding factor as to whether or not I believe you. If you tell me you want to be about God's business but never have a dime to put in an offering or have to be sternly cajoled every time it's offering time, then that tells me you aren't as serious about God's business as you claim. If you've got money for things such as family events, special nights out, new outfits, new hairstyles, new cars, and for activities that are deemed "fun" but never seem to get around to making the offering you promised or developing the money for spiritual things (even for yourself), that tells me right there that your heart isn't with God as much as you might think it is. Protest all you like – money speaks louder than words. If you never have money for anything related to spiritual matters, then your heart is not in the Kingdom.

IS GOD REALLY FIRST?

I think we've created confusion when it comes to finances today because we give a lot of contradictory messages about where God is in our lives. We'll say that God should be first, but then we also say our spouses, our households, our jobs, our families, our leaders, and our ministries should be first, too. This creates confusion because…well…which is it? What is really supposed to be first in our lives, and how do we display that it's first?

Exodus 20:2-3: *I AM THE LORD YOUR GOD, WHO RESCUED YOU FROM THE LAND OF EGYPT, THE PLACE OF YOUR SLAVERY. YOU MUST NOT HAVE ANY OTHER GOD BUT ME.*

Matthew 6:33: *SEEK THE KINGDOM OF GOD ABOVE ALL ELSE, AND LIVE RIGHTEOUSLY, AND HE WILL GIVE YOU EVERYTHING YOU NEED.*

Matthew 10:37-39: *IF YOU LOVE YOUR FATHER OR MOTHER MORE THAN YOU LOVE ME, YOU ARE NOT WORTHY OF BEING MINE; OR IF YOU LOVE YOUR SON OR DAUGHTER MORE THAN ME, YOU ARE NOT WORTHY OF BEING MINE. IF YOU REFUSE TO TAKE UP YOUR CROSS AND FOLLOW ME, YOU ARE NOT WORTHY OF BEING MINE. IF YOU CLING TO YOUR LIFE, YOU WILL LOSE IT; BUT IF YOU GIVE UP YOUR LIFE FOR ME, YOU WILL FIND IT.*

John 3:30: *HE MUST BECOME GREATER AND GREATER, AND I MUST BECOME LESS AND LESS.*

Romans 8:5: *THOSE WHO ARE DOMINATED BY THE SINFUL NATURE THINK ABOUT SINFUL THINGS, BUT THOSE WHO ARE CONTROLLED BY THE HOLY SPIRIT THINK ABOUT THINGS THAT PLEASE THE SPIRIT.*

Simply put, the One Who is first in your life should be, before anyone and anything else, God. This means: your family, your job, your household, your spouse, your leader, and yes, even your ministry are not first. This might sound confusing, especially when we start talking about priorities and prioritizing. What do we do first if God is first? How do we handle God being first, and how do we display that?

God is to be first in our lives because without God, we don't have life, and we don't have the myriad of different things in our lives that we often want to prioritize as being "first." Without God, you don't have your marriage, your household, your job, your kids, your spiritual leaders, or the ministry you either run or are a part of in your local area. It's a matter of recognizing God's existence before we start breaking into the essence that is often our lives, and keeping that basic grounding above and before we endeavor to do anything else. Acknowledging God's presence gives us a sense of purpose, of worship, and of gratitude for all we go through in our days. It helps us to be thankful when things are going good, bad, or in between, and to handle the everyday stressors and difficulties that come along with maintaining and living and balancing life.

Yet I meet way too many Christians who are seriously out of balance when it comes to life. They have difficulty handling the stresses of life, especially financial difficulties. They spend their money on all of the things that come from God: their households, bills, children, spouses, the personal needs of their spiritual leaders, going to and from their jobs, or yes, even on their ministries. I've even met Christians who are retired and living on their own, divulging large sums of money to their adult children who are taking advantage of them and nothing more. Then when it's time to give – either to the leader who covers and guides you, to another ministry that's struggling or in straits, to help build the ministry they are a part of or are growing themselves, to missions, or to anything extra – they don't give. They claim their money went to family, which is seen as an acceptable, non-arguable excuse, even though the situations surrounding the dispensation of income are not honorable. Or maybe it went to a personal, non-essential need, for them or someone else; to bills, when overspending is involved; to a special event with their spouse; to something job-related; or something, they claim, that was to the benefit of themselves and what they want to do.

It is true that we can't give to every cause and need in existence, but what I described above is wrong, for multiple reasons. The first reason it is wrong is because it is based on excuses and lies that are created by society. When they come up, people are telling us that something else was more important. Money clarifies we have the money for what is important to us – and if giving and spending on all these other things comes first – then the Kingdom isn't that important to that individual. We can make all the excuses we want. If you aren't giving and are never able to give to the Kingdom, then God is not first in your life, something else is. If this is the case, it is time to step back and reevaluate the idolatry that has taken over your life, why it's there…and change it.

FINDING A REASONABLE BALANCE

A lot of people believe the Bible introduces contradictions; I believe it introduces balance. The different perspectives that the Bible provides prove to us that different circumstances exist, and that one answer is not the same in every single situation. There isn't a right or a wrong way to have a life; only wrong ways to live out one's life. God doesn't expect us to erase our needs or to give so much that we can't live efficient lives. This is one of the first arguments I usually encounter when it comes to giving, and pressing upon people to give. I believe in every country in the world, despite income, we all have something we can give monetarily to God. None of us should be constantly taking and others always giving. The Kingdom of God requires all of us, and all of us need to be able to take objective inventory of our lives and our financial situations in order to be better givers when it comes to the Kingdom.

Catch is, none of us really likes parting with our money. We like to have money to do what we want to do with it, and we don't like the idea that God not only asks us to give financially; He point blank expects it of us. Not giving financially is not an option. Sometimes I think this makes us more inclined to have an attitude or excuse when it comes to not giving, especially when we can make it sound altruistic and sacrificial.

- "God wouldn't ask these children to go without, would He?"
- "But my husband and I need time to ourselves to develop our marriage – and we all know He cares about marriage, right?"
- "But I'm overworked and deserve to take this time for myself!"

The problem with these statements is that they are said in such a way that challenges God's Word to us about finances. God's precepts about giving are very clear and no, He doesn't expect that your children should go without, that you never take time for your marriage, or that you never do anything for yourself. These statements reflect that such individuals have lives that are already out of balance, and their finances are displaying it. When they get caught, they want to make it sound like their money is overextended and is needed elsewhere, not for God's direct work or for His spiritual household.

God can't be expected to understand month after month when it comes to financial mismanagement. We all know that things come up from time to time that are emergency situations or stretch us a little too thin, but this can't be a constant state of being. His work can't take the hit because there are too many things that you are putting before Him in your life. These are situations that require a re-orientation of priorities, and getting real with self and God, admitting that when it comes to giving, there are things that are coming before God that shouldn't.

1 Timothy 3:5: *FOR IF A MAN CANNOT MANAGE HIS OWN HOUSEHOLD, HOW CAN HE TAKE CARE OF GOD'S CHURCH?*

We use the above passage to reference the work of bishops, but the truth of it pertains to all of us who claim to be Christians and are called to care for the church from a financial perspective. If we are out of balance in our personal lives, we aren't going to be able to care for the church, either. Being balanced means setting priorities. If giving to God is required first, then that means it has to come before everything else financially laid out each month. If we find ourselves expecting God to get the short end of that stick, we need to look at just where we are spending our money and what is keeping us from being financially available for His service.

WHERE DO PEOPLE SPEND THEIR MONEY?

I have said for years that I refuse to believe that people have "no money." Someone, somewhere in this world has a lot more money than we might have, but we all have some money. People might not want to spend their money, they might not want to give it to your cause, or they might have it allotted elsewhere, but it's not that they don't have any money. Saying they have "no money" is in the hopes that you will believe that statement and not persist in requesting it from them anymore.

How do I know this? Because the statistics on spending state otherwise. There is always money for things that people WANT to spend their money on. Seeing the realities of just what we are spending our money on annually in black and white are actually quite staggering.

- Tobacco products: $35 billion[1]
- Beer: $100 billion[2]
- Marijuana products: $10-120 billion[3]
- Plastic surgery: $12 billion[4]
- Ice cream: $13.7 billion[5]
- Smartphones: $108 billion[6]
- Eating out at restaurants: $50 billion[7]
- Going to the movies: $29 billion[8]
- Gambling: $34.6 billion[9]
- Guns and ammunition: $15 billion[10]
- St. Patrick's Day: $4.14 billion[11]
- Costumes: $310 billion[12]
- Pet costumes: $51 billion[13]
- Chocolate: $16 billion[14]
- Perfume: $4.2 billion[15]
- Taxidermy: $800 million[16]
- Soft drinks: $65 billion[17]
- Fast food: $117 billion[18]
- Credit card late fees: $18 billion[19]
- Ringtones: $5 billion[20]

- Lawn care: $40 billion[21]
- Video games: $17 billion[22]
- Professional sports: $25.4 billion[23]

When we look over this vast list of items, it should be sobering to see not just how much money is spent, but how many of these things we ourselves have either bought or somehow participated in the economy thereof to drive up the annual revenue for these products. When I originally found a list for this while doing the original manuscript on this work back in 2004, the numbers for the majority of these items that were also on the list were in the millions – not billions. That means between now and 2004, we have increased our spending on these items in the amounts of billions of dollars annually. That's scary when you think about it. It tells us where the hearts of people are, where their priorities lie and that the majority of the things they seek in this life are simply not necessities.

Mark 8:36-37: *AND WHAT DO YOU BENEFIT IF YOU GAIN THE WHOLE WORLD BUT LOSE YOUR OWN SOUL? IS ANYTHING WORTH MORE THAN YOUR SOUL?*

It's not wrong to do something special every now and then or to enjoy things in life. I myself indulge in some of the things on this list from time to time. The issue is when having these things consumes one's life over good sense and having these things – the aspirations of a lifestyle – comes before God in your life. We might not want to admit it, but an awful lot of us are chasing after these things in the hopes that God will understand and will prosper us...and then we are confused and discouraged when He does not.

HOLDING ON TO THINGS YOU DON'T NEED

One of the biggest ways we lose money is by holding onto things that have become idols in our lives. They might not have started out that way, but over time, we've come to associate something with things that we are unwilling to let go. Whether we hold on to them to compete with others, out of emotional sentimentality, not to lose face, or to prove something to ourselves, we often hear God telling us to let go of things and hold onto them long after doing so is not financially profitable.

For example: there are millions of Americans who live in homes they cannot reasonably afford. Maybe at one time they required the size of the house they are now living in (sometimes that's not even the case), but their circumstances have since changed. Children grew up and left home, maybe someone got divorced, maybe someone died. Incomes changed with the downturn of the economy a few years ago and they aren't pulling in the same amount of profit that they used to. The house they live in is a financial burden, something that sucks large amounts of their financial resources...for no justifiable reason, at all.

There are also millions of Americans who pay out high payments monthly to pay for a car that has already lost a third of its value just driving it off the car lot. It's possible, even easier, to cover the cost of a used car that is just as functional, but instead of doing this, they pay out nearly double the value of the car in order to have a new one. Sometimes they aren't doing this with just one car, but two or three at a time, when there is no reason to have so many vehicles to begin with.

The examples I have given are clear cases of living beyond one's means to hold onto things that aren't really needed. Yes, we all need somewhere to live and living in the United States often requires one to have a personal vehicle for transportation, but there is absolutely no reason why finding something smaller, more affordable, used, or consolidated isn't an option. The only reason this option is often not examined is because the people involved protest or will not hear of it, and do so unreasonably. They have more than they need, more than they can handle, and more than their finances allow, yet they don't let it go because they are holding on for wrong reasons.

1 Corinthians 10:13: *THE TEMPTATIONS IN YOUR LIFE ARE NO DIFFERENT FROM WHAT OTHERS EXPERIENCE. AND GOD IS FAITHFUL. HE WILL NOT ALLOW THE TEMPTATION TO BE MORE THAN YOU CAN STAND. WHEN YOU ARE TEMPTED, HE WILL SHOW YOU A WAY OUT SO THAT YOU CAN ENDURE.*

The Bible teaches us that God doesn't give us more than we can handle, and that means He is not going to tempt us. The issues we have with temptation aren't unique to us, and we can trust that God is faithful toward us in all things. We apply this verse in an emotional and spiritual sense, but it can apply in a practical sense, as well.

If we can't afford the car, the house, the additional bills, the credit card debt, and the multiple monthly payments to do something, then God isn't in it. It's also perfectly possible that God did give us something for a season or to get us through a season in our lives, but that the season is now up and it's time to move past it so we can receive new blessings in our lives that we won't be able to obtain if we keep holding onto old things.

Many people could find a greater prosperity and not only have more to give, but more to live off of and use for experiences if they would let go of things that are weighing them down. Looking over life, finding a way to reduce required overhead expenses, and removing things from our lives that no longer serve our needs and have become a burden is just a better way to be throughout life.

MONEY AND GOVERNANCE

I believe one of the reasons we have many financial problems goes back to governance issues. We have grown accustom to convenience and luxuries, and we don't realize that everything we encounter is not a necessity. As a result, we often attribute much of where we are to the will of God, upset by inconvenience, thinking we need to spend more money to attain "need," when what we are really seeking after is comfort and convenience.

Joshua 24:15: *BUT IF YOU REFUSE TO SERVE THE LORD, THEN CHOOSE TODAY WHOM YOU WILL SERVE. WOULD YOU PREFER THE GODS YOUR ANCESTORS SERVED BEYOND THE EUPHRATES? OR WILL IT BE THE*

GODS OF THE AMORITES IN WHOSE LAND YOU NOW LIVE? BUT AS FOR ME AND MY FAMILY, WE WILL SERVE THE LORD.

Proverbs 16:9: *WE CAN MAKE OUR PLANS, BUT THE LORD DETERMINES OUR STEPS.*

God does not stand over us with a whip. He gives us the option of free will, free expression, and yes, free governance. It is our responsibility to follow out His commands in our life and it is our responsibility to make sure we handle and govern our lives accordingly. This principle of governance is often taught improperly or not taught at all, which leaves a void in our understanding of responsibility of all sorts. Yes, it is fine to see God at work in one's life and it is awesome to see His hand moving as we walk through and work out different circumstances and situations. This doesn't mean we are all just mere chess pawns without any say or thought in our decision-making. God's governance means that we have the ability to examine our situations and make responsible choices, and not only should we exercise that responsibility, we are expected to as believers. In governance, we are called to figure out the differences in the following five experiences:

- I want...
- I think...
- I feel...
- I perceive...
- I need...

To effectively govern, you need to recognize the differences in these things in your lives. If you mistake need with want or feelings with need, your finances are going to forever take a serious beating. Yes, sometimes when we clean up our finances or manage them well, we are in situations where we feel uncomfortable. We might not like what we are asked to live with and we might wish we had something else. Tithing might not be fun, but God still requires it. Being serious about Kingdom giving may very well mean living with less or doing something different to change your financial situation. Nonetheless, governance helps us to distinguish genuine want from genuine need. If we are going to be good stewards, we have to recognize the difference between the two and refrain from being financially impulsive.

In other words: it's time to grow up when it comes to money and take control of financial situations. God calls us to be responsible, not wistful, with our money. The devil doesn't make you spend too much money; you make you spend too much money. Yes, things are expensive, but you don't have to buy so many things. Yes, you might have days where you are upset, but your feelings shouldn't require you to spend money you don't have. Self-discipline starts when we accept our governing role in our lives and stop blaming everyone and everything else for our financial states.

ARE YOU BEING ATTACKED?

One of the most common prayer requests I receive is for a perceived "financial attack" to end. When I ran a regular prayer line, somewhere in the ballpark of 90% of prayer requests were for financial matters. I would say somewhere around 50% of those calls would specifically request prayer for a "financial attack" in one form or another. These requests indicated that the person making the request believed the following:

- They didn't have enough money to do something they wanted to do.
- They believed that, as a result, they were experiencing a demonic attack.
- They believed that praying over the situation would resolve it.

I don't know the situations of every single person who made these requests, but I did meet some of them after the fact well enough to know that the situation behind the scenes wasn't as super-spiritual as they led us all to believe. The majority of time, the reality was actually quite practical:

- They overspent on something, such as a trip or other luxury, and were now short to make ends meet at the end of the month.
- They wanted to make a special offering to something, but didn't have the money left at the end of the month to do so after paying for other things.

- They didn't budget or didn't know how to budget.
- They were in debt and tired of being in debt.

The truth is that while I don't question the enemy can attack our finances, he doesn't do it by himself. Remember, where our treasure is, our heart is there, also! What we choose to buy or spend is our choice, whether it is godly or not. It reveals more about us and our own spiritual states than it does about spiritual attacks in our lives. The enemy comes in and moves through our decisions to overspend or to stretch ourselves too thin because we don't accept governance of our finances. A lot of the time we get financially attacked, we open the door wide and willing for the enemy to waltz in and before we know it, our money is being shelled out to creditors, retailers, and debtors for things we don't need and shouldn't be entertaining.

Psalm 37:21: *THE WICKED BORROW AND NEVER REPAY, BUT THE GODLY ARE GENEROUS GIVERS.*

It's fine to pray for your finances, but it's time to stop praying for financial miracles. The financial miracle that is needed is your own dedication and obedience to govern your finances properly. We can't ask God to take our responsibility for this most vital area in our lives and erase our mismanagements. Instead of praying that attacks go away, pray that God will show you how to better handle your finances so attacks don't happen.

HAVING A WILLING HEART

Sometimes we don't give because we refuse to see ourselves through to do it. We insist we can't afford it, don't have the money for it, and the only reason for it is we just don't want to do it. Whether it's for all the reasons we have explained or something more, the attitude of our hearts is wrong and the Kingdom pays the price for it.

Ephesians 4:1-6: *THEREFORE I, A PRISONER FOR SERVING THE LORD, BEG YOU TO LEAD A LIFE WORTHY OF YOUR CALLING, FOR YOU HAVE BEEN CALLED BY GOD. ALWAYS BE HUMBLE AND GENTLE. BE PATIENT WITH EACH OTHER, MAKING ALLOWANCE FOR EACH OTHER'S FAULTS BECAUSE OF YOUR LOVE. MAKE EVERY EFFORT TO KEEP YOURSELVES UNITED IN THE SPIRIT, BINDING YOURSELVES TOGETHER WITH PEACE. FOR THERE IS ONE BODY AND ONE SPIRIT, JUST AS YOU HAVE BEEN CALLED TO ONE GLORIOUS HOPE FOR THE FUTURE. THERE IS ONE LORD, ONE FAITH, ONE BAPTISM, ONE GOD AND FATHER OF ALL, WHO IS OVER ALL, IN ALL, AND LIVING THROUGH ALL.*

We talk all the time about unity and presenting a more united front in Christianity, working through our differences and considering the needs of others. One of the most important ways we accomplish this is not through talking about it, but by supporting one another in our Kingdom work. In comparison with the flourishing industries we spoke of earlier, the following statistics reveal where churches are at today:

- More than 4,000 churches close annually.[24]
- Every year, 2.7 million church members go inactive.[25]
- 70% of pastors feel grossly underpaid.[26]
- 90% of pastors report working between fifty-five and seventy-five hours each week.[27]
- 50% of ministers starting out will not last in ministry five years.[28]
- The profession of "pastor" is near the bottom of a survey of the most respected professions. It is just above "car salesman."[29]

Some of those billions of dollars we discussed earlier are being spent by Christians who are nothing more than unwilling to give in the way they should for the advance of the Kingdom. The heart of these issues lie in an unwillingness to be a part of the church and unify with it in the way we should. If we are truly believers, we recognize God has connected us to the Body of Christ in such a way that we can't keep disconnecting our time, our lives, and yes, our finances from it. There should be no question that churches remain functioning, missionaries continue to go out, and ministries continue to grow. This can't happen, however, if the finances just aren't there because they are being spent on other things.

This is the precise reason why Jesus told us outright that wherever our money is, there our heart is. Thus, let's be real and admit the following statements are true:

- If you are willing to pay $3,000 for concert tickets, then your heart is with that concert or that artist.
- If you are willing to pay several hundred dollars for shoes, then your heart is with those shoes.
- If you are willing to pay a ridiculous amount of money for a car that you don't even need, then your heart is with that car.
- If you want to keep a house you can't afford, then your heart is with that house.
- If you want to spend money on luxuries on a regular basis and don't make priorities in your life, then your heart is with those luxuries.
- If you keep bailing irresponsible family and friends out of their financial situations, or give everyone what they want all the time, without question, then your heart is with those people and those situations.
- If you want to skimp on offerings to the church or refuse to give, then that tells us your heart is not with the church.

In other words, stop lying and saying you don't have the money when it's offering time! A good minister can tell where your heart is at and you can't keep saying you love God the most or first and have money for everything EXCEPT the Kingdom of God! If you believe in it, then you have to put your money where your mouth is and make it the priority!

JOURNALING

- Is God first in your life? Answer this question seriously, considering the information presented in this chapter.
- How can you find better balance when it comes to your giving and spending?
- What do you recognize about governance, and how can better governance help you with your finances?
- How can you attune yourself to be more willing to give to the things of God?

References

[1]http://www.worldlungfoundation.org/ht/display/ReleaseDetails/i/20439/pid/6858. Accessed on May 2, 2016.
[2]http://www.huffingtonpost.com/2012/02/14/us-beer-sales_n_1276300.html. Accessed May 2, 2016.
[3]http://www.cnbc.com/id/36179677. Accessed May 2, 2016
[4]http://pattmd.com/cosmetic-surgery-2/much-america-spend-plastic-surgery/. Accessed May 2, 2016
[5]http://fortune.com/2014/07/24/ice-cream-sales/. Accessed May 2, 2016
[6]http://www.deathandtaxesmag.com/200611/how-much-do-americans-really-spend-on-their-iphones/. Accessed May 2, 2016
[7]http://www.eater.com/2015/3/6/8163891/americans-spend-more-restaurants-grocery-stores. Accessed May 2, 2016.
[8]http://www.cinemablend.com/new/Global-Audiences-Spent-Record-Breaking-Amount-Money-Movies-2015-103737.html. Accessed May 2, 2016.
[9]http://mentalfloss.com/article/31222/numbers-how-americans-spend-their-money. Accessed May 2, 2016.
[10]http://www.marketwatch.com/story/10-things-the-gun-industry-wont-tell-you-2014-03-07. Accessed May 2, 2016.
[11]http://mentalfloss.com/article/31222/numbers-how-americans-spend-their-money. Accessed May 2, 2016.
[12]http://mentalfloss.com/article/31222/numbers-how-americans-spend-their-money. Accessed May 2, 2016.
[13]http://mentalfloss.com/article/31222/numbers-how-americans-spend-their-money. Accessed May 2, 2016.

[14]http://mentalfloss.com/article/31222/numbers-how-americans-spend-their-money. Accessed May 2, 2016.
[15]http://mentalfloss.com/article/31222/numbers-how-americans-spend-their-money. Accessed May 2, 2016.
[16]http://mentalfloss.com/article/31222/numbers-how-americans-spend-their-money. Accessed May 2, 2016.
[17]http://mentalfloss.com/article/31222/numbers-how-americans-spend-their-money. Accessed May 2, 2016.
[18]http://mentalfloss.com/article/31222/numbers-how-americans-spend-their-money. Accessed May 2, 2016.
[19]http://mentalfloss.com/article/31222/numbers-how-americans-spend-their-money. Accessed May 2, 2016.
[20]http://mentalfloss.com/article/31222/numbers-how-americans-spend-their-money. Accessed May 2, 2016.
[21]http://mentalfloss.com/article/31222/numbers-how-americans-spend-their-money. Accessed May 2, 2016.
[22]http://mentalfloss.com/article/31222/numbers-how-americans-spend-their-money. Accessed May 2, 2016.
[23]http://mentalfloss.com/article/31222/numbers-how-americans-spend-their-money. Accessed May 2, 2016.
[24]http://www.churchleadership.org/apps/articles/default.asp?articleid=42346&columnid=4545. Accessed May 2, 2016.
[25]http://www.churchleadership.org/apps/articles/default.asp?articleid=42346&columnid=4545. Accessed May 2, 2016.
[26]http://www.pastoralcareinc.com/statistics/. Accessed May 2, 2016.
[27]http://www.pastoralcareinc.com/statistics/. Accessed May 2, 2016.
[28]http://www.pastoralcareinc.com/statistics/. Accessed May 2, 2016.
[29]http://www.pastoralcareinc.com/statistics/. Accessed May 2, 2016.

4 GIVING AND SPENDING ACCORDING TO BIBLE PRINCIPLES

IN order to gain a balanced perspective on financial giving and on financial responsibility, we have to see for ourselves what the Bible teaches us about these things. We often hear terms such as "tithe," "offering," "giving" "debt," and "applying faith to finances" thrown around, but we don't often understand just what they mean or what they are speaking of. While this chapter is nowhere near the entirety of what the Bible has to say about money, it is an overview, if you will, of a personal guide to approaching finances with faith as simply as possible.

GIVE, AND IT SHALL BE GIVEN UNTO YOU

Giving is a basic Biblical principle. Most people

only apply giving to the monetary sense but giving is the action of providing a gift in any form – financial, material, spiritual, or emotional – given from one person to another or from a person to God, or from God to another person. It can be for a special purpose (such as a birthday, anniversary, or other event), or to celebrate something (a friendship, a relationship, or a date), or just to bless someone else, with no special occasion or formal reason. Giving also includes donations of material goods or foodstuffs to organizations geared toward providing for those who lack basic material things necessary for the sustenance of life.

Deuteronomy 10:18: *HE ENSURES THAT ORPHANS AND WIDOWS RECEIVE JUSTICE. HE SHOWS LOVE TO THE FOREIGNERS LIVING AMONG YOU AND GIVES THEM FOOD AND CLOTHING.*

If we are Christians, we are required to give. We are required to give of ourselves, we are required to give of our time, we are required to give of our bounty (such as things for the needy) and we are required to give of our finances. From a young age, children should be taught to give, both to the church and to others. As adults, we should make sure giving is a priority, and something that we make a focal point in our lives. It is something we can all do, young or old, rich or poor, male or female. Even though this book is specifically about finances, we should never get it in our minds that all we have to do is give to others through money. We should also be people who reach out when people are hurting, volunteer our time and do things for others without cost, offer kind words, and ensure that we make sure we know how to give more than just our money.

Mark 12:41-44: *JESUS SAT DOWN NEAR THE COLLECTION BOX IN THE TEMPLE AND WATCHED AS THE CROWDS DROPPED IN THEIR MONEY. MANY RICH PEOPLE PUT IN LARGE AMOUNTS. THEN A POOR WIDOW CAME AND DROPPED IN TWO SMALL COINS. JESUS CALLED HIS DISCIPLES TO HIM AND SAID, "I TELL YOU THE TRUTH, THIS POOR WIDOW HAS GIVEN MORE THAN ALL THE OTHERS WHO ARE MAKING CONTRIBUTIONS. FOR THEY GAVE A TINY PART OF THEIR SURPLUS, BUT SHE, POOR AS SHE IS, HAS GIVEN EVERYTHING SHE HAD TO LIVE ON."*

Luke 6:38: *GIVE, AND YOU WILL RECEIVE. YOUR GIFT WILL RETURN TO YOU IN FULL – PRESSED DOWN, SHAKEN TOGETHER TO MAKE ROOM FOR MORE, RUNNING OVER, AND POURED INTO YOUR LAP. THE AMOUNT YOU GIVE WILL DETERMINE THE AMOUNT YOU GET BACK.*

I state all of this because it's important that, when we approach giving in all its different forms (but especially money) we don't do it with the agenda to always get something back. Just as the poor widow gave because it was the right thing to do, so too are we expected to do the same. God does promise us that we will receive for what we give, but nowhere in Scripture does He promise we will always receive back monetarily. What we are promised is that the cycle of giving goes on and continues, and if we want to see God's system work, we have to take the initiative to make sure we are giving like we should, from start to finish, in every way possible.

TITHING

Tithing tends to be controversial sport when it comes to giving, especially among churchgoers who teach it to be a part of the law. In a certain sense, they are correct in assigning a tithe with legalities: Israel was an ancient nation, with laws, rules, and borders, and tithing was also an ancient form of taxation. In fact, tithing was not unique to the ancient Hebrews. It was a taxation system put into place to make sure that ancient governments received ten percent of everyone's bounty, income, and harvest before any other monies, funds, or expenses were addressed. This gave governments the security of that guaranteed income, not allowing anyone to say they didn't have the money or couldn't provide their taxes, because the money was taken first.

Tithing, however, is something that goes beyond the ancient law of Israel that we find in the Old Testament. The way it was applied in Israel was a little unique, but it was present prior, nonetheless. Tithing as a governmental principle predates the written law, as we can see between Melchizedek, King of Salem, and Abram:

Genesis 14:20: *THEN ABRAHAM GAVE MELCHIZEDEK A TENTH OF ALL THE GOODS HE HAD RECOVERED.*

Under the Old Covenant, the tithe benefited the Levites, who were the priests involved in offering the regular sacrifices in the temple. The Levites did not receive a land inheritance as part of their arrangement, and this meant that the people's tithes gave them the ability to live, survive, and thrive as they offered this important service for the people of ancient Israel. Obviously a type for our five-fold ministers today, the direct benefit of the Levites' reception of tithes didn't nullify that the tithe was given to God. It just clarifies that tithing benefited those who kept God's service in operation, and was used for the purpose of temple upkeep, the lives of spiritual leaders, and for the needed maintenance in both life and building of spiritual places.

To understand tithing now for the Christian, tithing is the taxation system for the Kingdom of God. If we call ourselves believers, that means we are a part of God's Kingdom, and God's Kingdom requires that its needs this side of heaven are provided for. As the citizens of the Kingdom, our tithe, or ten percent of our income, goes back to God first, before we spend any other money for anything else. If we offer nothing else to the Kingdom, our tithe is that required first ten percent to ensure the Kingdom of God can keep going. Contrary to popular belief, evidence and support for tithing is found in the New Testament, by Jesus Himself:

Matthew 23:23: *WHAT SORROW AWAITS YOU TEACHERS OF RELIGIOUS LAW AND YOU PHARISEES. HYPOCRITES! FOR YOU ARE CAREFUL TO TITHE EVEN THE TINIEST INCOME FROM YOUR HERB GARDENS, BUT YOU IGNORE THE MORE IMPORTANT ASPECTS OF THE LAW – JUSTICE,*

MERCY, AND FAITH. YOU SHOULD TITHE, YES, BUT DO NOT NEGLECT THE MORE IMPORTANT THINGS.

Before you balk at the idea of having to give God ten percent of your income, consider the fact that governmental taxes today are far higher than a mere ten percent. In most countries, government taxes are anywhere from thirty to fifty percent of a person's income, so God could be asking a lot more of us than He is. In His wisdom, He recognizes that if everyone will contribute ten percent of their income, the Kingdom can function rightly and we will be able to maintain our churches and our leaders who devote their entire lives to church service.

Tithes prove that the people of God who serve in full-time ministry should be able to do their ministry work with pure devotion, without having to maintain a secular job to do so. This, unfortunately, has become a breakdown in our churches today because people do not want to get behind the vision of the leader long enough or with enough enthusiasm to tithe regularly. Amidst cries that leaders should have to work like everyone else, leaders are devoting more and more time to secular jobs in order to keep churches going because they cannot provide for themselves, their families, or the maintenance of their ministry without doing so. This simply should not be and is a sign that we aren't following God's financial precepts in church. Making sure that the church and its leaders are provided for without question is a part of God's system, and a sign that not only do we honor the leader's commitment to that ministry, we also honor God at work within that leader. By refusing to tithe regularly, we refuse to honor the complete Kingdom function that He has established. By tithing regularly, we raise it up and prove to God that we trust His Kingdom and His purposes.

On another note: the tithe you pay to your church or ministry isn't yours; it has been given to God. You have no right to try and run the church or ministry from the pew because you have given your tithe. Tithe payers don't have the right to dictate how the tithe is used, because that shows a lack of trust in both God and the leader you sit under, as God has called them. Being a tithe payer means having a good attitude, doing so cheerfully, and doing so without a hidden side or secretive need for control through that money.

Tithing shows that God is most important in our lives and that we are seeking first the Kingdom of God before we seek our own benefit. As a result, those who tithe are blessed of God, because they are seeing to it that the priorities of seeking first the things of God are met.

Leviticus 27:30: *ONE-TENTH OF THE PRODUCE OF THE LAND, WHETHER GRAIN FROM THE FIELDS OR FRUIT FROM THE TREES, BELONGS TO THE LORD AND MUST BE SET APART TO HIM AS HOLY.*

Deuteronomy 10:14: *LOOK, THE HIGHEST HEAVENS AND THE EARTH AND EVERYTHING IN IT ALL BELONG TO THE LORD YOUR GOD.*

Deuteronomy 14:22-23: *YOU MUST SET ASIDE A TITHE OF YOUR CROPS – ONE-TENTH OF ALL THE CROPS YOU*

HARVEST EACH YEAR. BRING THIS TITHE TO THE DESIGNATED PLACE OF WORSHIP – THE PLACE THE LORD YOUR GOD CHOOSES FOR HIS NAME TO BE HONORED – AND EAT IT THERE IN HIS PRESENCE. THIS APPLIES TO YOUR TITHES OF GRAIN, NEW WINE, OLIVE OIL, AND THE FIRSTBORN MALES OF YOUR FLOCKS AND HERDS. DOING THIS WILL TEACH YOU ALWAYS TO FEAR THE LORD YOUR GOD.

Proverbs 3:9: *HONOR THE LORD WITH YOUR WEALTH AND WITH THE BEST PART OF EVERYTHING YOU PRODUCE.*

Thus we are able to see that tithing does meet a practical need, but it also meets and provides a spiritual need in our lives. As it shows God most important in our lives, we are able to establish a good sense of spiritual order within our personal disciplines, especially those that relate to finances. It proved that as all one had comes from the land, the ability to work the land and all that is in it came first from God. We can see commitment from tithing and that God is not just for the Sabbath, Sunday, or the day of the week when people went to church, but for all of their days. It proves God is with us in all of our labors. The practical purpose of the tithe was to keep the temple running and provide payment to the Levites, who worked to operate the temple and its sacrifices, since they did not receive the same inheritance as the other tribes. Therefore, the purposes of the tithe are the same as they were in days of old: to give back to God, to show our priorities, our commitments, and to ensure that those in the church and who spread the Gospel are able to do so and earn a living at the same time.

A word of important note about tithing: tithes are paid to either a church or ministry that is meeting your spiritual needs on a regular basis and instructing you and others in the Word. If you are a minister yourself, your tithe should be paid into the church or ministry that is your spiritual leader's organization. Tithes are not for the operation of general charitable or general religious organizations, and should be reserved for only those places that feed you spiritually. Tithes should, likewise, not be sent to television preachers, missionaries, or general ministers that you do not have a spiritual teaching relationship with.

Tithing is an opening to blessing from God, both those who benefit from the tithes by hearing the Word, those who benefit by being able to live off the tithes, and you, the presenter of the tithe, too!

OFFERING

The Bible doesn't just mention one type of offering. There are, in fact, multiple forms of offering in the Bible. The five major offerings found in the Old Testament are:

- **Burnt offering (Leviticus 1)** – Completely consumed on the altar, nothing eaten by human beings.
- **Meal offering (Leviticus 2)** – Offering made without the shedding of blood and without

an animal sacrifice, offered of very fine flour
- **Peace offering (Leviticus 3)** – Offering where the one making the offering can eat the meat of the sacrifice, for fellowship or communion
- **Sin offering (Leviticus 4)** – Required offering, relating to sin and the problems related to sin
- **Trespass offering (Leviticus 5)** – Required offering, dealing with specific sins

There were five different animals used in offerings:

- Oxen
- Sheep
- Goats
- Pigeons
- Turtledoves

We can understand an offering to be any form of giving to the Kingdom of God that falls outside of tithing. There are two major differences between a tithe and a general offering. The first is that a tithe is specifically ten percent of one's income, while an offering can be more or less than that amount. The second is that a tithe specifically goes into the ministry that you are directly receiving from, while an offering can be for or can go to something else. Offerings might also be related to bringing forth reparation for something, making something right, or setting something on a good path. Offerings might be for a special church project, a specific social Gospel ministry, a missionary or visiting minister, a Christian school, a charitable organization, a building fund, a new church, or a television ministry or minister, paralleling the concept of offerings for specific projects.

Exodus 25:2: *TELL THE PEOPLE OF ISRAEL TO BRING ME THEIR SACRED OFFERINGS. ACCEPT THE CONTRIBUTIONS FROM ALL WHOSE HEARTS ARE MOVED TO OFFER THEM.*

Offerings are also not always monetary, as we can see from the list above and the examples above. We can make offerings in the form of goods, food, time, supplies, equipment, or other forms of service.

The principle of the offering teaches us that tithing is not the end of giving, but the beginning of it. While tithing is the first financial priority, we are also reminded that we should make special provision for offerings, as well. Offerings connect us to the church universal, reminding us that church is bigger than just the one local church or ministry we might sit under. Offerings provide for travelling preachers, for those who do work within the community that is not directly related to preaching, and ensures that those who do work and labors beyond weekly services receive the provision and funding needed to complete works from start to finish.

THE BIBLE AND DEBT

We can't talk about the Bible's precepts on money and not discuss debt. Debt is the result of financial spending beyond one's means, where one owes far more than they can financially pay back, causing the borrower to become the slave to the lender, and gaining new debt because of the inability to pay it back as a result.

Deuteronomy 24:16: *TRUE JUSTICE MUST BE GIVEN TO FOREIGNERS LIVING AMONG YOU AND TO ORPHANS, AND YOU MUST NEVER ACCEPT A WIDOW'S GARMENT AS SECURITY FOR HER DEBT.*

1 Samuel 22:2: *THEN OTHERS BEGAN COMING – MEN WHO WERE IN TROUBLE OR IN DEBT OR WHO WERE JUST DISCONTENTED – UNTIL DAVID WAS THE CAPTAIN OF ABOUT 400 MEN.*

Proverbs 11:15: *THERE'S DANGER IN PUTTING UP SECURITY FOR A STRANGER'S DEBT; IT'S SAFER NOT TO GUARANTEE ANOTHER PERSON'S DEBT.*

Proverbs 17:18: *IT'S POOR JUDGMENT TO GUARANTEE ANOTHER PERSON'S DEBT OR PUT UP SECURITY FOR A FRIEND.*

Proverbs 27:13: *GET SECURITY FROM SOMEONE WHO GUARANTEES A STRANGER'S DEBT. GET A DEPOSIT IF HE DOES IT FOR FOREIGNERS.*

Matthew 18:23-34: *"THEREFORE, THE KINGDOM OF HEAVEN CAN BE COMPARED TO A KING WHO DECIDED TO BRING HIS ACCOUNTS UP TO DATE WITH SERVANTS WHO HAD BORROWED MONEY FROM HIM. IN THE PROCESS, ONE OF HIS DEBTORS WAS BROUGHT IN WHO OWED HIM MILLIONS OF DOLLARS. HE COULDN'T PAY, SO HIS MASTER ORDERED THAT HE BE SOLD—ALONG WITH HIS WIFE, HIS CHILDREN, AND EVERYTHING HE OWNED—TO*

PAY THE DEBT. "BUT THE MAN FELL DOWN BEFORE HIS MASTER AND BEGGED HIM, 'PLEASE, BE PATIENT WITH ME, AND I WILL PAY IT ALL.' THEN HIS MASTER WAS FILLED WITH PITY FOR HIM, AND HE RELEASED HIM AND FORGAVE HIS DEBT. "BUT WHEN THE MAN LEFT THE KING, HE WENT TO A FELLOW SERVANT WHO OWED HIM A FEW THOUSAND DOLLARS. HE GRABBED HIM BY THE THROAT AND DEMANDED INSTANT PAYMENT. "HIS FELLOW SERVANT FELL DOWN BEFORE HIM AND BEGGED FOR A LITTLE MORE TIME. 'BE PATIENT WITH ME, AND I WILL PAY IT,' HE PLEADED. BUT HIS CREDITOR WOULDN'T WAIT. HE HAD THE MAN ARRESTED AND PUT IN PRISON UNTIL THE DEBT COULD BE PAID IN FULL. "WHEN SOME OF THE OTHER SERVANTS SAW THIS, THEY WERE VERY UPSET. THEY WENT TO THE KING AND TOLD HIM EVERYTHING THAT HAD HAPPENED. THEN THE KING CALLED IN THE MAN HE HAD FORGIVEN AND SAID, 'YOU EVIL SERVANT! I FORGAVE YOU THAT TREMENDOUS DEBT BECAUSE YOU PLEADED WITH ME. SHOULDN'T YOU HAVE MERCY ON YOUR FELLOW SERVANT, JUST AS I HAD MERCY ON YOU?' THEN THE ANGRY KING SENT THE MAN TO PRISON TO BE TORTURED UNTIL HE HAD PAID HIS ENTIRE DEBT."

Debt is not new, even though we do sometimes treat it as if it is a new, modern idea. Throughout the Bible, we see examples of borrowers and lenders, and individuals who made a living off the profit of poor individuals who got into debt and had no way out. It is something that has followed individuals around for thousands of years because debt creates a huge profit for wealthy conglomerates and institutions as people pay back what they owe, plus interest. It's a dirty, exploiting cycle that people turn to for a variety of reasons, but all of which remain the same way.

In the Old Testament, the Israelites practiced a principle known as the Year of Jubilee, which was observed every fifty years in order to forgive debts, free slaves and prisoners, and to rest the land from harvesting. It was what we might call a "sabbatical year," one in which the different issues that plagued a nation and could cause serious issues if left unchecked were released and forgiven.

Leviticus 25:8-13: *IN ADDITION, YOU MUST COUNT OFF SEVEN SABBATH YEARS, SEVEN SETS OF SEVEN YEARS, ADDING UP TO FORTY-NINE YEARS IN ALL. THEN ON THE DAY OF ATONEMENT IN THE FIFTIETH YEAR, BLOW THE RAM'S HORN LOUD AND LONG THROUGHOUT THE LAND. SET THIS YEAR APART AS HOLY, A TIME TO PROCLAIM FREEDOM THROUGHOUT THE LAND FOR ALL WHO LIVE THERE. IT WILL BE A JUBILEE YEAR FOR YOU, WHEN EACH OF YOU MAY RETURN TO THE LAND THAT BELONGED TO YOUR ANCESTORS AND RETURN TO YOUR OWN CLAN. THIS FIFTIETH YEAR WILL BE A JUBILEE FOR YOU. DURING THAT YEAR YOU MUST NOT PLANT YOUR FIELDS OR STORE AWAY ANY OF THE CROPS THAT GROW ON THEIR OWN, AND DON'T GATHER THE GRAPES FROM YOUR UNPRUNED VINES. IT WILL BE A JUBILEE YEAR FOR YOU, AND YOU MUST KEEP IT HOLY. BUT YOU MAY EAT WHATEVER THE LAND PRODUCES ON ITS OWN. IN THE YEAR OF JUBILEE EACH OF YOU MAY RETURN TO THE LAND THAT BELONGED TO YOUR ANCESTORS.*

The Year of Jubilee hasn't been practiced as a general rule in thousands of years, but it does show that debt was a problem, even in ancient times. In the New Testament, we also see debt and how debt was handled, with specific injunctions in the New Testament to avoid debt, all together.

Romans 13:7-8: *GIVE TO EVERYONE WHAT YOU OWE THEM: PAY YOUR TAXES AND GOVERNMENT FEES TO THOSE WHO COLLECT THEM, AND GIVE RESPECT AND HONOR TO THOSE WHO ARE IN AUTHORITY. OWE NOTHING TO ANYONE – EXCEPT FOR YOUR OBLIGATION TO LOVE ONE ANOTHER. IF YOU LOVE YOUR NEIGHBOR, YOU WILL FULFILL THE REQUIREMENTS OF GOD'S LAW.*

There is a reason why the Bible tells us that we should owe no debt to one another, except love, and that reason can be seen all the way back in the principles about the Year of Jubilee: debt was long associated with slavery. In ancient times, inability to pay back a loan led an individual right into enslavement. As Christians who are called to be free, we know the Bible did not overthrow every single social situation in place at the time, and slavery was no exception. Being advised to avoid debt, however, was wise because debt introduced an inequality into the church, giving other believers the "upper hand," so to speak, over others in the Body of Christ. This led to contention, to improper conduct, and any other number of issues that would make someone feel unwelcome in their own church.

DEALING WITH DEBT

I want to say right off the bat: not all acquired debt is irresponsibly gained. There are situations where medical emergencies or accidents arise, thus causing people to incur thousands of dollars in medical debt in a single instant. Sometimes people lose jobs and fall behind on bills, through no fault of their own. Yes, there are people who are irresponsible with credit cards and reckless spending, but that isn't every single case of debt that exists in this world. It's a myth that people who have debt are always lazy, irresponsible, or financially wild. Sometimes life happens, debt pops up, and there are always people in this world who are eager and willing to take advantage of bad situations that happen throughout life from time to time.

Debt is the ugly secret in many Christians' closets. It usually stays in their closets because people are embarrassed or ashamed to be open about their debts. With new converts every day, more and more people are joining the family of God with pasts that just don't disappear at the Sinner's Prayer and that require serious examination and repair over time. There are also many Christians who acquire debt through life, as we discussed in the last paragraph. Then there are many Christians who, due to the expenses of life and the pursuit of industry (the commercialism of Christianity, often done by many ministries) where millions of Christians have misused or are continuing to misuse credit and debit cards, internet buying, and spending excessively beyond their means. Debt is a serious problem, causing the cause of Christ to suffer, the families to suffer, and the course of a family's life to change, most often, in a permanent manner.

Proverbs 3:6: *SEEK HIS WILL IN ALL YOU DO, AND HE WILL SHOW YOU WHICH PATH TO TAKE.*

The simple answer: if you don't want debt, don't get into debt, is a simple solution to a problem that isn't always that simple. There are solid ways that we can avoid debt that are within our control, which we should seek to do in accordance with the Christian life. These means are:

- No gambling
- No lottery tickets
- No illegal drugs
- Do not misuse credit or debit cards
- Curbing internet buying
- No unnecessary spending
- Staying within a reasonable means of what you can afford

In a more practical sense, this often means disciplining one's self when it comes to money: buying the used car instead of leasing a new one, buying a smaller home instead of a larger and more expensive one, and perhaps doing without extravagant vacations, toys your children do not need, new electronics every year, and excessive holiday and birthday celebrations. It is an adjustment when overspending has been present, but it is a far easier adjustment to make than the feeling of drowning in debt.

This advice is just as applicable for those who are in debt as those who desire to avoid it. Even though it might not erase the debt you already have, it can help prevent new debt and allow additional finances to pay off existing debt.

I would love to tell you that if you send me a certain amount of money, I will wave a magic wand over your picture and debt situation and it will all just magically disappear, but that wouldn't be honest of me. I can tell you that I will pray for your debt and your situation, but I can't guarantee for you that it will just magically go away. Just like anything in our lives that we get into, we have to put forth some effort to get out of financial debt. Whether we are in it through our own fault or not, we can depend on God to help us to get out of it so we can move forward with our lives.

First things with debt are first: examine the situation and pray about it. Denial isn't going to fix your problem. You need to sit down either by yourself (if you are single) or as a couple and gather all the tangible signs of debt and figure out just how deep in debt you are so you can know just how far you have to come out of it. Then, once you have an accurate picture of the situation, you must pray for guidance and direction about it.

The second step is, after prayer, putting your debt into proper believer's perspective. Being in debt does not give you *carte blanche* to back out on your God-ordained responsibilities like tithing, mortgage payments, repaying debts, or paying taxes. God is still first, and we need to keep our commitments to God and to give God what belongs to Him. We should also avoid bankruptcy, if it is possible. The Bible encourages us to repay our debts, and we should do our best to be faithful. The reason for this advice is just as much for us as for

Biblical principle. When we declare bankruptcy or refuse to pay a debt, it causes interest rates, fees, and other things to increase for everybody. Whether acquired fairly or not, it isn't prudent to cause additional long-term expense to one's self or to others. Being irresponsible about debt – no matter how it is acquired – is not going to solve the problems debt creates.

Step number three is to work out a budget, which is a prepared statement each month of your income, your outgo, and the necessary income needed in order to maintain your life each month. I am not going to get into a long dissertation on budgeting, because there are numerous books and internet advisers who give advice on budgeting, which, as a rule, is not that hard to do. Many of the resources professionals offer on budgeting are free. In order to properly budget, you need to know how much money comes into your household each month and how much you spend on various expenses. A simple chart can be created in a program such as Microsoft Excel or in various software programs, all of which make budgeting easy and simple to follow.

Whether you create a budget yourself from scratch or you use existing software programs or book legers to maintain your finances, a budget is the most important tool you can have to maintain financial responsibility. When you don't know what your regular spending habits are, it's a lot easier to be irresponsible with money. Budgeting is a time-honored practice held by those who are in debt and not in debt alike, and it is the best way to keep track of financial situations and know what to expect from month-to-month.

The fourth step is to eliminate "debt tempters" in your life once you see for yourself where your money is being spent and start embracing the principle of greater discipline with finances, wherever possible. If you can't handle having them responsibly, the credit cards have to go. Anything that has the temptation to be mishandled financially has to leave your life until you are in a position to better manage it. Go back to doing things the old fashioned way: pay cash where possible or use a debit card that immediately deducts funds rather than giving a grace period to repay funds. Don't be frivolous with your money. Skip the vacation, the outfit, the new car, or the special event you cannot afford and wait until you can afford it. Learn how to manicure your own fingernails and dye your own hair. As more time goes by, learn about the basics of discount buying (you can find excellent, brand-new suits and clothing on sites such as eBay and other sites for extremely reasonable prices), and don't spend all your time trying to keep up with everyone else or outdoing your neighbors.

In other words, be creative! Getting out of debt doesn't mean the end of life, it means being more selective about how you live life so you can enjoy it more. Nobody likes the idea of living with the constant threat of creditors, debtors, and interest over their heads. Debt reduction is, for most people, not a quick fix or something that happens all at once. It starts as one smaller bill is paid off in full, and then larger ones also start getting paid off, one at a time. Eventually, over time we are able to be financially free, without the sting of debt hanging over our heads.

INTRODUCING FAITH-BASED FINANCES

When I first started out in ministry some years ago, God challenged me to approach my finances in a different way than was popular at the time. Coupling the principles of budgeting with the principles of God, I had a tendency to be a little on the stingy side. I felt like there was never enough money to do anything and that meant I wasn't apt to spend money because I was afraid I wouldn't have enough money for something else.

What God challenged me to do was be led of my finances by the Holy Ghost, just as I was led by the Holy Ghost in other areas of my life. Just like I prayed about whether or not to take a preaching engagement or whether or not to write a new book, I started praying as to whether or not I should buy something or I should wait. It might sound funny, but what it has led me to is being able to know when God is in something as pertains to spending and when He is not. I call it the principle of faith-based finances, because I am using my faith to help me handle my money in the best possible way.

Faith-based finances is a principle of living where your faith determines how you spend. It is the financial aspect of learning to be led by the prompting of the Holy Ghost in your life toward decisions that are either helpful or away from those that are harmful. As this book has illustrated, it isn't God's will for His children to live on the edge of financial ruin or drowning in debt for even a part of their lives. This means that He wants to guide us into all levels of financial success and that if we tune into Him, and follow all of His financial precepts, He will guide us through the Holy Ghost just as He does on any other area of our lives. So on every major purchase or decision and even sometimes on those that aren't so major, God is there, and we need to be paying good enough attention to know how He is guiding us.

Sometimes God's guidance comes through nothing more than good old-fashioned common sense. If you can't afford the SUV and don't need the SUV then you shouldn't get yourself into debt by buying the SUV. If you can buy the same exact shoes at Wal-Mart for a fraction of the price, it isn't worth it to overspend for a designer name. If it seems totally unreasonable, it isn't a good idea and if it seems to be a potential for debt, it's not God encouraging you to make that purchase.

However, we live in an age where many of us tend to go the other direction: we literally have to be forced to spend money, make purchases, or give to God. For fear that money will dry up or disappear, too many people live bound by the fear of spending money or making purchases even with God's prompting or blessing. This kind of lifestyle is just as detrimental as overspending without God's providence. Faith-based finances may in this case be God instructing someone to make a purchase and then trust Him for the ability to pay for it. Whatever our issues are with money, and even if we don't have any at all, faith-based finances is the surest way to balance out this very important area of our lives. Matthew 6:20-21 provides the very good words, which even though we have looked at prior in this book, we are going to look at here, again:

STORE YOUR TREASURES IN HEAVEN, WHERE MOTHS AND RUST CANNOT DESTROY, AND THIEVES DO NOT BREAK IN AND STEAL. WHEREVER YOUR TREASURE IS, THERE THE DESIRES OF YOUR HEART WILL ALSO BE.

Using God's guidance ensures us that we shall put Him first in all financial things, always make wise financial choices, and most importantly, lay up treasure in heaven, some of which might be showered down this side of heaven, proving once and for all that all our needs can be met through God.

Another principle of faith-based finances is sowing and reaping in the sense that we are forever sowing in preparation for God's harvest in both our lives and however it manifests. Yes, we do sow at church, and we do sow when we give in the Kingdom, but we also sow whenever we do or purchase something that is a part of our future in the Kingdom, in the ministry, or in our lives, in general. If we are always investing in what God desires us to invest in, then we know everything that we do shall touch the Kingdom and shall bring us to a greater sense of His constant presence in our lives.

The more we give, within reason and without neglect to practical financial matters, the more God will bless us. Because finances are a part of our lives, the amount of generosity we display in one part shows how generous we are in other parts of our lives as well. We should be willing to give to God at all times and on all occasions when He requires giving beyond our tithe, and not live stingy lives but those that overflow to Him, that He may give back to us even more, and we can give back even more to support the cause of Jesus Christ.

JOURNALING

- Why is giving important for Christians?
- What did you learn about tithing from this chapter?
- What did you learn about offerings from this chapter?
- What attitude should we take toward debt?
- Create a budget for yourself. What are you able to see from your budget about your financial situation?

5 PROSPERITY...OR SOMETHING LIKE IT

PROSPERITY is one of those topics that I have gone back and forth on over the years. The truth is that I have heard preachers who preached on prosperity in such a way that I wanted to believe them and believe that financial matters were as simplistic as they said, in the same manner and system that they talked about. I would listen to how they would preach on it and I wanted to believe it so much, that it was so simple, that I tried my very best to adopt the system myself, within my own life. I have also gone to the opposite end of the extreme, where I believed that prosperity did not exist in any form and that it was not a part of anything Biblical, nor any semblance of anything right.

When I originally wrote the basic booklet that has become this book, I was trying very hard to convince myself that I could find something redemptive in prosperity teaching. The truth is that I since have, but it's not in quite the way that I originally wrote it, nor is it the way that it is typically taught. I would like to hope that what I present here will be a more balanced approach to the prosperity issue, avoiding the temptation to claim prosperity as a "right," but also avoid the temptation to abandon the concept all together.

PROSPERITY AS A PROBLEMATIC DOCTRINE

I have nothing against the concept of prosperity as a principle. I think that describing prosperity as the fullness of life God desires us to have is a fine way of thinking. There's no problem with seeing it as a way to approach financial matters that can increase and benefit one's economic state. To me, prosperity is about far more than money, but I will speak on this a little later in this chapter. I think that if we understand prosperity properly, it introduces us to a world of spiritual economy, one where we trust and rely on God to provide our needs rather than the world. It's a fine idea, it's a fine concept, and it's something that, if we understand the concept of the Kingdom of God as more than just a nice idea, can bless us in our lives and help us to have a great attitude about life and giving throughout our spiritual walk.

The problem I have with prosperity is when it is treated as a fundamental doctrine of Christianity, on par with the salvation of Christ, the Fatherhood of God, the sanctification of the Holy Ghost, the unity of the Godhead, and the other core teachings that we hold at the base of our spiritual belief system. I have seen financial prosperity listed in the statement of faith or mission statements of many churches, listed alongside the inspiration of the Scriptures and the atoning work of the Lord. To me, this is a bit much; this is treating prosperity as something it was never intended to become, and making it something that is a core understanding of our faith, when it is, in fact, a peripheral.

Truth be told, prosperity was never something deemed so important throughout much of our Christian history. Whether we always agree with the formation of the church in ancient times is not of consequence; the reality is that prosperity was not ever something on the radar. In reality, it was often something that was shunned, something regarded as a luxury that led to evil, and people who were willing to forsake all their earthly goods were regarded as holier and more upstanding than those who sought after many worldly possessions.

Do I believe the extreme perspective Christians had about money in past years is extreme? Yes, I certainly do. I acknowledge that while we are living on this earth, we do need things to survive, such as food and shelter, and I also recognize that the basic economic needs of Christians vary from nation to nation. At the same time, I can't deny that I feel we have swung to the extreme opposite end of the spectrum when it comes to prosperity, feeling like we have gone from extreme, strict disciplines that don't serve a purpose to lavish living, also without a purpose.

Prosperity taught as a doctrine has several problematic implications. It does nothing to teach us about the principle of wealth (being truly prosperous, or blessed) and being rich (having and enjoying an undisciplined cash flow). The first, and probably most important, is that how much money someone has is equated with their level of faith. It's assumed that if you are experiencing financial lack or going through a difficult period of time from an economic perspective that you are experiencing that because you don't have enough faith in a certain area. This is absurd for more than one reason. There is nowhere in Scripture, nor in history, for that matter, where people's faith was measured by their income. This is an elitist idea, one that demoralizes individuals in poorer countries as well as demoralizing the poor everywhere, and makes it seem as if Christianity is a promise for wealthy people rather than one for everyone.

Proverbs 22:2: *THE RICH AND POOR HAVE THIS IN COMMON: THE LORD MADE THEM BOTH.*

Matthew 5:45: *IN THAT WAY, YOU WILL BE ACTING AS TRUE CHILDREN OF YOUR FATHER IN HEAVEN. FOR HE GIVES HIS SUNLIGHT TO BOTH THE EVIL AND THE GOOD, AND HE SENDS RAIN ON THE JUST AND UNJUST ALIKE.*

I believe that God can and does provide for His people, but I also believe that, as the Bible states, it rains on the just and the unjust alike. Good things happen to good people and bad alike, bad things happen to good people and bad alike, and money happens to both believers and non-believers. To measure the spiritual by the material is not a Biblical precept, and it introduces economic competition in the church, whereas people use materialism to flaunt and put one another down.

Akin to the issue of measuring faith via funds is the issue that people are now always constantly trusting or believing God for more money. The reason for this is simple: if money is a measure of one's faith, then money is where the increase of faith will be seen. I've gone from seeing the majority of believers trust God for healing or their unsaved relatives to seeing request after request after request for more money, all on the guise that they need to have it as a part of being believers. The problem with this mentality becomes when is enough, enough? It would seem from many believers and teachers alike that there never seems to be an end in the wants of the church, and despite the promises that are made in conjunction with prosperity and giving, many believers are holding back funds because they don't think what they have is ever enough to give to anyone else.

Prosperity as a doctrine has created an inability to assess a true financial state among believers. We don't understand the difference between true lack and true want, and we claim to be "in lack" if our circumstances seem somehow inconvenient or uncomfortable to us. While people in other countries fall asleep in dirt huts without any food at all, we claim to be "in lack" if we aren't able to go out to a restaurant to eat or if we can't buy a new pair of shoes or a new set of golf clubs. It's absurd to compare such opulence with lack, but it shows the reality of where too many Christians are in their thinking. They don't realize just how much they have, they live in states of ingratitude because they think it is God's will they always have more, and they aren't thankful.

When people don't know how much they really have, they are not apt to give. If there's always more they think they SHOULD have, they don't want to give from what they DO have because they don't think it's enough. I see it over and over again in individuals who are always believing God for that next big financial breakthrough or financial miracle. They might have some money, but not thinking it's what they should have, they don't appreciate it. It's disregarded, and out the same window winds up giving, because if you don't think you have enough, you aren't apt to share.

Let me lay it out plain: if you can find money for a vacation, for things for yourself, for your children, for your cars, for your lives, for the "increase" you feel you are worthy of, you are neither in lack, nor in financial despair. You might not have as much as you might like to one day have, but having food, housing, and luxuries renders you far more fortunate than most in this world today. That being said, no matter how much you are vying to be financially prosperous, you can find the money to give to the Kingdom with the scenario I just laid out, and not just a little dollar here and there. As much as you invest in yourself, you can invest it in the Kingdom, too.

Acts 20:35: *AND I HAVE BEEN A CONSTANT EXAMPLE OF HOW YOU CAN HELP THOSE IN NEED BY WORKING HARD. YOU SHOULD REMEMBER THE WORDS OF THE LORD JESUS: "IT IS MORE BLESSED TO GIVE THAN TO RECEIVE."*

As Christians, we shouldn't have to cajole or make a bunch of promises to people in order to get them to give. There shouldn't be such a ridiculous process involved to try and get people to participate in Kingdom giving, and there should never, ever be a Christian who comes to church without at least a few dollars to give in the offering. Lack means having absolutely nothing, not being uncomfortable. Being prosperous means starting somewhere and starting with something, and it starts with being grateful, giving and sharing, and being a people who are balanced with finances.

BIBLICAL MODESTY

In the early church, there was serious cultural disparity between the wealthy and the poor. The wealthy were quick to flaunt their wealth, lord it over the poor, and expect preferential treatment for no other reason than they had money. The poor were often expected to take a back seat to the rich, and were treated as subordinates.

The answers to solve the problems resulting from this inequality between the poor and the rich are what we now know as Biblical teachings on modesty. Contrary to popular belief, Biblical modesty has absolutely nothing to do with sex, revealing clothing, enticing the opposite sex, or anything having to do with attractions of a physical nature. Biblical modesty was about money, and about dressing in such a way that made no class distinction between the rich and the poor. This one meant that the burden was on the rich to tone it down, to avoid the temptation to lord wealth over those who were not as well off economically.

Ezekiel 22:27: *YOUR LEADERS ARE LIKE WOLVES WHO TEAR APART THEIR VICTIMS. THEY ACTUALLY DESTROY PEOPLE'S LIVES FOR MONEY!*

Ezekiel 33:31: *SO MY PEOPLE COME PRETENDING TO BE SINCERE AND SIT BEFORE YOU. THEY LISTEN TO YOUR WORDS, BUT THEY HAVE NO INTENTION OF DOING WHAT YOU SAY. THEIR MOUTHS ARE FULL OF LUSTFUL WORDS, AND THEIR HEARTS SEEK ONLY AFTER MONEY.*

James 1:9-11: *BELIEVERS WHO ARE POOR HAVE SOMETHING TO BOAST ABOUT, FOR GOD HAS HONORED THEM. AND THOSE WHO ARE RICH SHOULD BOAST THAT GOD HAS HUMBLED THEM. THEY WILL FADE AWAY LIKE A LITTLE FLOWER IN THE FIELD. THE HOT SUN RISES AND THE GRASS WITHERS; THE LITTLE FLOWER DROOPS AND FALLS, AND ITS BEAUTY FADES AWAY. IN THE SAME WAY, THE RICH WILL FADE AWAY WITH ALL OF THEIR ACHIEVEMENTS.*

James 2:1-7: *MY DEAR BROTHERS AND SISTERS, HOW CAN YOU CLAIM TO HAVE FAITH IN OUR GLORIOUS LORD JESUS CHRIST IF YOU FAVOR SOME PEOPLE OVER OTHERS? FOR EXAMPLE, SUPPOSE SOMEONE COMES INTO YOUR MEETING DRESSED IN FANCY CLOTHES AND EXPENSIVE JEWELRY, AND ANOTHER COMES IN WHO IS POOR AND DRESSED IN DIRTY CLOTHES. IF YOU GIVE SPECIAL ATTENTION AND A GOOD SEAT TO THE RICH PERSON, BUT YOU SAY TO THE POOR ONE, "YOU CAN STAND OVER THERE, OR ELSE SIT ON THE FLOOR"—WELL, DOESN'T THIS DISCRIMINATION SHOW THAT YOUR*

JUDGMENTS ARE GUIDED BY EVIL MOTIVES? LISTEN TO ME, DEAR BROTHERS AND SISTERS. HASN'T GOD CHOSEN THE POOR IN THIS WORLD TO BE RICH IN FAITH? AREN'T THEY THE ONES WHO WILL INHERIT THE KINGDOM HE PROMISED TO THOSE WHO LOVE HIM? BUT YOU DISHONOR THE POOR! ISN'T IT THE RICH WHO OPPRESS YOU AND DRAG YOU INTO COURT? AREN'T THEY THE ONES WHO SLANDER JESUS CHRIST, WHOSE NOBLE NAME YOU BEAR?

1 Peter 3:3-4: *DON'T BE CONCERNED ABOUT THE OUTWARD BEAUTY OF FANCY HAIRSTYLES, EXPENSIVE JEWELRY, OR BEAUTIFUL CLOTHES. YOU SHOULD CLOTHE YOURSELVES INSTEAD WITH THE BEAUTY THAT COMES FROM WITHIN, THE UNFADING BEAUTY OF A GENTLE AND QUIET SPIRIT, WHICH IS SO PRECIOUS TO GOD.*

We can apply the economic lording of many prosperity preachers over those who follow them to be a flaunting of their wealth in direct contrast with the Biblical commands to modesty. Showing off excessive displays of wealth as some sort of a statement of faith is in direct disobedience to the Word the preachers claim to believe in. Beyond this, I think we need to face the reality that says there are only a few who "name it and claim" it, as we would say, as well as the prosperity concept in general, that it is working for. The rest of people are helping them to achieve their prosperous status, while losing their chance at it themselves. This should make us step back and think about prosperity, about modesty, and about our general relationship with money, especially given the limited results of such a teaching.

IF...THEN

What many don't teach is that prosperity as was understood in a Biblical sense was not without condition. It wasn't something that neither the Israelites, nor the church received freely, simply because they were believers. If anything, the church became a haven for both the rich and poor because it promised eternal benefits to everyone, regardless of income. This is not to say that the Israelites and the early church did not have the same opportunity to apply prosperity as a principle in their lives, but I would say that for much of the history of the early church, it wasn't the focus that it has become. In the early church, the church was intimately concerned with making sure as many people were prepared for the return of Christ, which they believed would happen in their lifetimes. As subsequent generations came and went, new priorities came about for the church, adapting to different cultures and different issues of the day.

This means that prosperity as we understand it today, as the emphasis is made today, is very much a western ideal, reflecting western culture and western concepts about money and wealth. It doesn't translate universally (beyond being a desire that most people have) and it doesn't translate throughout the different eras of church history. Thus, if we are going to truly understand prosperity in a Biblical sense, we have to take off our limited blinders that look only at it from our own immediate understanding and start to expand the understanding of it to bless us for all time.

I believe that we can define prosperity as a fullness, as a concept of the abundant life laid out in John 10:10, only in a more specified way. Deuteronomy 28, a sixty-eight verse chapter, lays out the conditions of prosperity, the blessings of being prosperous, and also the curses and punishments for disobeying God's commands and therefore not living in abundance. Verse 1 outlines the conditions:

Deuteronomy 28:1: *AND IT SHALL COME TO PASS, IF THOU SHALT HEARKEN DILIGENTLY UNTO THE VOICE OF THE LORD THY GOD, TO OBSERVE AND TO DO ALL HIS COMMANDMENTS WHICH I COMMAND THEE THIS DAY, THAT THE LORD THY GOD WILL SET THEE ON HIGH ABOVE ALL NATIONS OF THE EARTH...* (KJV)

So in other words, prosperity comes into our lives not simply because we accept Jesus, but because we listen to God's voice and observe His commandments to us. Prosperity is one of those "if/then" conditions of Scripture: If we do something, this results; and if we do not do it, there are consequences. It's something that we have to do something to obtain, and it's not something that everyone in Christianity finds, or always wants to find. Prosperity is a blessing and state of existence that we are given by God as a sign of the power and abundance available for those who obey Him, intended to make the world wonder what we have. It's the victorious reward, this side of heaven, for seeking something higher than earthly pursuits of money, gain, or self-indulgence. And the bottom line to prosperity is that we are either obeying God and living a full Christian life and experiencing the fullness of prosperity, or we aren't.

Deuteronomy 28:2-14: *...AND ALL THESE BLESSINGS SHALL COME ON THEE, AND OVERTAKE THEE, IF THOU SHALT HEARKEN UNTO THE VOICE OF THE LORD THY GOD. BLESSED SHALT THOU BE IN THE CITY, AND BLESSED SHALT THOU BE IN THE FIELD. BLESSED SHALL BE THE FRUIT OF THY BODY, AND THE FRUIT OF THY GROUND, AND THE FRUIT OF THY CATTLE, THE INCREASE OF THY KINE, AND THE FLOCKS OF THY SHEEP. BLESSED SHALL BE THY BASKET AND THY STORE. BLESSED SHALT THOU BE WHEN THOU COMEST IN, AND BLESSED SHALT THOU BE WHEN THOU GOEST OUT. THE LORD SHALL CAUSE THINE ENEMIES THAT RISE UP AGAINST THEE TO BE SMITTEN BEFORE THY FACE: THEY SHALL COME OUT AGAINST THEE ONE WAY, AND FLEE BEFORE THEE SEVEN WAYS. THE LORD SHALL COMMAND THE BLESSING UPON THEE IN THY STOREHOUSES, AND IN ALL THAT THOU SETTEST THINE HAND UNTO; AND HE SHALL BLESS THEE IN THE LAND WHICH THE LORD THY GOD GIVETH THEE. THE LORD SHALL ESTABLISH THEE AN HOLY PEOPLE UNTO HIMSELF, AS HE HATH SWORN UNTO THEE, IF THOU SHALT KEEP THE COMMANDMENTS OF THE LORD THY GOD, AND WALK IN HIS WAYS. AND ALL PEOPLE OF THE EARTH SHALL SEE THAT THOU ART CALLED BY THE NAME OF THE LORD; AND THEY SHALL BE AFRAID OF THEE. AND THE LORD SHALL MAKE THEE PLENTEOUS IN GOODS, IN THE FRUIT OF THY BODY, AND IN THE FRUIT OF THY CATTLE, AND IN THE FRUIT OF THY GROUND, IN THE LAND WHICH THE LORD SWARE UNTO THY FATHERS TO GIVE THEE. THE LORD SHALL OPEN UNTO THEE HIS GOOD TREASURE, THE HEAVEN TO GIVE THE RAIN UNTO THY LAND IN HIS SEASON, AND TO BLESS*

ALL THE WORK OF THINE HAND: AND THOU SHALT LEND UNTO MANY NATIONS, AND THOU SHALT NOT BORROW. AND THE LORD SHALL MAKE THEE THE HEAD, AND NOT THE TAIL; AND THOU SHALT BE ABOVE ONLY, AND THOU SHALT NOT BE BENEATH; IF THAT THOU HEARKEN UNTO THE COMMANDMENTS OF THE LORD THY GOD, WHICH I COMMAND THEE THIS DAY, TO OBSERVE AND TO DO THEM: AND THOU SHALT NOT GO ASIDE FROM ANY OF THE WORDS WHICH I COMMAND THEE THIS DAY, TO THE RIGHT HAND, OR TO THE LEFT, TO GO AFTER OTHER GODS TO SERVE THEM. (KJV)

Wow! That is a mouthful, right there. It's obvious that, as I have stated before, prosperity is about a lot more than a statement in a bank account according to the Bible. It's about more than money, paying bills, and buying stuff, but about the essence of being blessed of God. This passage alone shows us that we can be prosperous in many ways and that the fullness of God's prosperity rests in blessings in our lives, both natural and spiritual. His hand rests upon our lives, our families, our relationships, favor wherever we are – city or country, blessings of health, abundance when we do our jobs, safety from enemies, having more than enough to provide, being established as a blessed and holy people, being able to lend without having to borrow, and being placed in a position of primacy. What an incredible list for a great life! Deuteronomy 28 shows us what happens when we put God first and attune ourselves to obedience, following His precepts throughout our lives.

All this sounds good, and sounds like far more than we ever considered. However... we are reminded in the conclusion of the condition on prosperity: all this is conditioned that we observe the commands of God and essentially that we play by His rules. Jesus reminds us that if we truly love Him, we will obey His commands (John 14:15). It's not as simple as just saying you want to believe something or do something, it's actually doing it, putting it into practice whether you see the desired results immediately or not, and dedicating yourself to the Lord in a way that seeks His face rather than what He can give you.

The remaining verses in Deuteronomy 28 describe in graphic detail the opposite of the prosperous life, which is the disobedient life. Because of the length of this passage we will only have a few of the verses here to provide an image for a picture.

Deuteronomy 28:15-20,25,44-46: *BUT IT SHALL COME TO PASS, IF THOU WILT NOT HEARKEN UNTO THE VOICE OF THE LORD THY GOD, TO OBSERVE TO DO ALL HIS COMMANDMENTS AND HIS STATUTES WHICH I COMMAND THEE THIS DAY; THAT ALL THESE CURSES SHALL COME UPON THEE, AND OVERTAKE THEE: CURSED SHALT THOU BE IN THE CITY, AND CURSED SHALT THOU BE IN THE FIELD. CURSED SHALL BE THY BASKET AND THY STORE. CURSED SHALL BE THE FRUIT OF THY BODY, AND THE FRUIT OF THY LAND, THE INCREASE OF THY KINE, AND THE FLOCKS OF THY SHEEP. CURSED SHALT THOU BE WHEN THOU COMEST IN, AND CURSED SHALT THOU BE WHEN THOU GOEST OUT. THE LORD SHALL SEND UPON THEE CURSING, VEXATION, AND REBUKE, IN ALL THAT THOU SETTEST THINE HAND INTO FOR TO DO, UNTIL THOU BE DESTROYED; AND UNTIL THOU PERISH QUICKLY:*

BECAUSE OF THE WICKEDNESS OF THY DOINGS, WHEREBY THOU HAST FORSAKEN ME. THE LORD SHALL CAUSE THEE TO BE SMITTEN BEFORE THINE ENEMIES: THOU SHALT GO OUT ONE WAY AGAINST THEM, AND FLEE SEVEN WAYS BEFORE THEM: AND SHALT BE REMOVED INTO ALL THE KINGDOMS OF THE EARTH. HE SHALL LEND TO THEE, AND THOU SHALT NOT LEND TO HIM: HE SHALL BE THE HEAD, AND THOU SHALT BE THE TAIL. MOREOVER ALL THESE CURSES SHALL COME UPON THEE, AND SHALL PURSUE THEE, AND OVERTAKE THEE, TILL THOU BE DESTROYED; BECAUSE THOU HEARKENEDST NOT UNTO THE VOICE OF THE LORD THY GOD, TO KEEP HIS COMMANDMENTS AND HIS STATUTES WHICH HE COMMANDED THEE: AND THEY SHALL BE UPON THEE FOR A SIGN AND FOR A WONDER, AND UPON THY SEED FOR EVER... (KJV)

Clearly, prosperity is about so much, and most importantly, it is about being blessed in our relationship with God. If we aren't right with God, our lives show that condition ad that is why so many more verses are given to the condition of the absence of prosperity, because it's about much more than money. It's about being involved with the Most High God, receiving His provision as much as His perspective and His Word, and following all unto obedience in a deep and powerful way.

WHY DO SO MANY LIVE WITHOUT PROSPERITY?

Once upon a time, I had a friend who I was just in awe of. She had tons of preaching engagements. People really seemed to like her. She had no mortgage payment or rental payment every month, and that was just beyond me. She was free to come and go as she pleased. Oh yeah, she was also flat broke, all the time.

It didn't make sense to me then; it doesn't make sense to me now. This is a good example, however, of where we are on matters of money in church, all-too-often. She might have believed in being rich and having a cash flow, but couldn't hold on to the cash she had. She didn't understand true prosperity and being able to live beyond money, and as a result, she never had any.

As a principle, I think people don't rightly understand prosperity. If you've never heard about it, then it's not something you will live and apply. If you have heard about prosperity in a wrong way, then you might think you are pursuing it, but you won't see it manifest as you hope. There are also people who just don't see it as a priority or in conflict with issues and perspectives they may have as Christians, and I do want to say that if that is the case, it is all right, in a certain sense. Some people are more concerned with having less because they have already been in position to have more, and they aren't interested in the weight and responsibility that having things or many people in their lives afford. While I do agree that a right understanding of prosperity can help them in whatever it is they want to do, there are many people who find the abundant life of Christ in a different way, and in different pursuits, than those specifically understood in prosperity teaching.

Genesis 12:2: *I WILL MAKE YOU INTO A GREAT NATION. I WILL BLESS YOU AND MAKE YOU FAMOUS, AND YOU WILL BE A BLESSING TO OTHERS.*

Luke 6:22: *WHAT BLESSINGS AWAIT YOU WHEN PEOPLE HATE YOU AND EXCLUDE YOU AND MOCK YOU AND CURSE YOU AS EVIL BECAUSE YOU FOLLOW THE SON OF MAN.*

Ephesians 3:6: *AND THIS IS GOD'S PLAN: BOTH GENTILES AND JEWS WHO BELIEVE THE GOOD NEWS SHARE EQUALLY IN THE RICHES INHERITED BY GOD'S CHILDREN. BOTH ARE PART OF THE SAME BODY, AND BOTH ENJOY THE PROMISE OF BLESSINGS BECAUSE THEY BELONG TO CHRIST JESUS.*

Revelation 21:7: *ALL WHO ARE VICTORIOUS WILL INHERIT ALL THESE BLESSINGS, AND I WILL BE THEIR GOD, AND THEY WILL BE MY CHILDREN.*

I also believe that many live without prosperity because they simply haven't been taught how to be responsible with it. When it comes to money, wrong motives, living according to certain precepts, and obedience, there are a lot of people who trip up in a major way. We often do things with motives, rather than just the pure love and joy of God, and that doing what we do with expectation causes us to lose the blessing associated and attached to it. God knows our hearts. He knows if we are genuinely seeking to be a blessing and walk rightly in Christian obedience to Him or if we are just doing things because we want something new to happen in our lives. Doing things with wrong motives (i.e., outside of God's will) means that we will reap no harvest from our giving. We cannot be doing because we just want to get a reward, however it may come, be it from the praise and acclamation of men or because we want a new outfit.

God wants us to be prosperous but because it is met with conditions in the Bible, we have to reach out and want it enough to meet the conditions by which we are promised prosperity. It's not just something we get from God; rather, it is something we are, because we love and obey Him.

JOURNALING

- Having seen the Biblical teaching on prosperity, what do you think of prosperity now?
- How did this study on prosperity change your views on Biblical modesty?

6 THE MINOR PROPHETS ON MONEY

A book that looks at finances from the perspective of a mission isn't complete unless we look at what the Minor Prophets had to say about money. While many books address the different visions of money across different books of the Bible, the Minor Prophets held some pretty strong words and ideas about money in general that we should hear to balance our views as believers.

It's not a secret that we live in a very materialistic world and that materialism has filtered down into our concepts about money in church. An interesting look at money, particularly to counter-balance a lot of the attitudes we hear now, is found in the words of some of the Minor Prophets, particularly those of Amos, Micah, Habakkuk, Haggai, and Malachi.

AMOS

Amos wasn't someone that anyone would have considered a likely candidate for the prophetic office. He was a shepherd and fig farmer from Judah, without any prophetic training or connection to the era's School of the Prophets. He was a simple man, one who was completely on the outskirts of formalize religion in his day. Regardless of this fact, Amos was God's choice, in his day, to proclaim a word to Israel that related to the ways that the people of God were unjust, especially in connection with their finances and treatment of those who are poor.

Amos 1:3-2:16: *THIS IS WHAT THE LORD SAYS: "THE PEOPLE OF DAMASCUS HAVE SINNED AGAIN AND AGAIN, AND I WILL NOT LET THEM GO UNPUNISHED! THEY BEAT DOWN MY PEOPLE IN GILEAD AS GRAIN IS THRESHED WITH IRON SLEDGES. SO I WILL SEND DOWN FIRE ON KING HAZAEL'S PALACE, AND THE FORTRESSES OF KING BEN-HADAD WILL BE DESTROYED. I WILL BREAK DOWN THE GATES OF DAMASCUS AND SLAUGHTER THE PEOPLE IN THE VALLEY OF AVEN. I WILL DESTROY THE RULER IN BETH-EDEN, AND THE PEOPLE OF ARAM WILL GO AS CAPTIVES TO KIR," SAYS THE LORD. THIS IS WHAT THE LORD SAYS: "THE PEOPLE OF GAZA HAVE SINNED AGAIN AND AGAIN, AND I WILL NOT LET THEM GO UNPUNISHED! THEY SENT WHOLE VILLAGES INTO EXILE, SELLING THEM AS SLAVES TO EDOM. SO I WILL SEND DOWN FIRE ON THE WALLS OF GAZA, AND ALL ITS FORTRESSES WILL BE DESTROYED. I WILL SLAUGHTER THE PEOPLE OF ASHDOD AND DESTROY THE KING OF ASHKELON. THEN I WILL TURN TO ATTACK EKRON, AND*

THE FEW PHILISTINES STILL LEFT WILL BE KILLED," SAYS THE SOVEREIGN LORD. THIS IS WHAT THE LORD SAYS: THE PEOPLE OF TYRE HAVE SINNED AGAIN AND AGAIN, AND I WILL NOT LET THEM GO UNPUNISHED! THEY BROKE THEIR TREATY OF BROTHERHOOD WITH ISRAEL, SELLING WHOLE VILLAGES AS SLAVES TO EDOM. SO I WILL SEND DOWN FIRE ON THE WALLS OF TYRE, AND ALL ITS FORTRESSES WILL BE DESTROYED." THIS IS WHAT THE LORD SAYS: "THE PEOPLE OF EDOM HAVE SINNED AGAIN AND AGAIN, AND I WILL NOT LET THEM GO UNPUNISHED! THEY CHASED DOWN THEIR RELATIVES, THE ISRAELITES, WITH SWORDS, SHOWING THEM NO MERCY. IN THEIR RAGE, THEY SLASHED THEM CONTINUALLY AND WERE UNRELENTING IN THEIR ANGER. SO I WILL SEND DOWN FIRE ON TEMAN, AND THE FORTRESSES OF BOZRAH WILL BE DESTROYED." THIS IS WHAT THE LORD SAYS: "THE PEOPLE OF AMMON HAVE SINNED AGAIN AND AGAIN, AND I WILL NOT LET THEM GO UNPUNISHED! WHEN THEY ATTACKED GILEAD TO EXTEND THEIR BORDERS, THEY RIPPED OPEN PREGNANT WOMEN WITH THEIR SWORDS. SO I WILL SEND DOWN FIRE ON THE WALLS OF RABBAH, AND ALL ITS FORTRESSES WILL BE DESTROYED. THE BATTLE WILL COME UPON THEM WITH SHOUTS, LIKE A WHIRLWIND IN A MIGHTY STORM. AND THEIR KING AND HIS PRINCES WILL GO INTO EXILE TOGETHER," SAYS THE LORD. THIS IS WHAT THE LORD SAYS: "THE PEOPLE OF MOAB HAVE SINNED AGAIN AND AGAIN, AND I WILL NOT LET THEM GO UNPUNISHED! THEY DESECRATED THE BONES OF EDOM'S KING, BURNING THEM TO ASHES. SO I WILL SEND DOWN FIRE ON THE LAND OF MOAB, AND ALL THE FORTRESSES IN KERIOTH WILL BE DESTROYED. THE PEOPLE WILL FALL IN THE NOISE OF BATTLE, AS THE WARRIORS SHOUT AND THE RAM'S HORN SOUNDS. AND I WILL DESTROY THEIR KING AND SLAUGHTER ALL THEIR

PRINCES," SAYS THE LORD. THIS IS WHAT THE LORD SAYS: "THE PEOPLE OF JUDAH HAVE SINNED AGAIN AND AGAIN, AND I WILL NOT LET THEM GO UNPUNISHED! THEY HAVE REJECTED THE INSTRUCTION OF THE LORD, REFUSING TO OBEY HIS DECREES. THEY HAVE BEEN LED ASTRAY BY THE SAME LIES THAT DECEIVED THEIR ANCESTORS. SO I WILL SEND DOWN FIRE ON JUDAH, AND ALL THE FORTRESSES OF JERUSALEM WILL BE DESTROYED." THIS IS WHAT THE LORD SAYS: "THE PEOPLE OF ISRAEL HAVE SINNED AGAIN AND AGAIN, AND I WILL NOT LET THEM GO UNPUNISHED! THEY SELL HONORABLE PEOPLE FOR SILVER AND POOR PEOPLE FOR A PAIR OF SANDALS. THEY TRAMPLE HELPLESS PEOPLE IN THE DUST AND SHOVE THE OPPRESSED OUT OF THE WAY. BOTH FATHER AND SON SLEEP WITH THE SAME WOMAN, CORRUPTING MY HOLY NAME. AT THEIR RELIGIOUS FESTIVALS, THEY LOUNGE IN CLOTHING THEIR DEBTORS PUT UP AS SECURITY. IN THE HOUSE OF THEIR GODS, THEY DRINK WINE BOUGHT WITH UNJUST FINES. "BUT AS MY PEOPLE WATCHED, I DESTROYED THE AMORITES, THOUGH THEY WERE AS TALL AS CEDARS AND AS STRONG AS OAKS. I DESTROYED THE FRUIT ON THEIR BRANCHES AND DUG OUT THEIR ROOTS. IT WAS I WHO RESCUED YOU FROM EGYPT AND LED YOU THROUGH THE DESERT FOR FORTY YEARS, SO YOU COULD POSSESS THE LAND OF THE AMORITES. I CHOSE SOME OF YOUR SONS TO BE PROPHETS AND OTHERS TO BE NAZIRITES. CAN YOU DENY THIS, MY PEOPLE OF ISRAEL?" ASKS THE LORD. "BUT YOU CAUSED THE NAZIRITES TO SIN BY MAKING THEM DRINK WINE, AND YOU COMMANDED THE PROPHETS, 'SHUT UP!' "SO I WILL MAKE YOU GROAN LIKE A WAGON LOADED DOWN WITH SHEAVES OF GRAIN. YOUR FASTEST RUNNERS WILL NOT GET AWAY. THE STRONGEST AMONG YOU WILL BECOME WEAK. EVEN

MIGHTY WARRIORS WILL BE UNABLE TO SAVE THEMSELVES. THE ARCHERS WILL NOT STAND THEIR GROUND. THE SWIFTEST RUNNERS WON'T BE FAST ENOUGH TO ESCAPE. EVEN THOSE RIDING HORSES WON'T BE ABLE TO SAVE THEMSELVES. ON THAT DAY THE MOST COURAGEOUS OF YOUR FIGHTING MEN WILL DROP THEIR WEAPONS AND RUN FOR THEIR LIVES," SAYS THE LORD.

Amos worked prophetically in an interesting way: he started out by saying things that would have clearly made those who received the message cheer loudly and with great enthusiasm. They would have automatically believed God would side with them, condemn their enemies, and cheer them on to victory. What they received instead was the complete opposite: God made it explicitly clear that the things Israel was doing were not any more acceptable in His sight than what their neighbors were doing. If anything, it was worse, because they knew better. They became people who were unjust, who did not do things according to God's precepts. One of the prime ways Israel was guilty of injustice was through exploitation of the poor and unfairly using manipulative tactics to steal from those who were less fortunate.

Through speaking passionately on injustice, particularly financial injustice, Amos gives us powerful insight into deep aspects of the prophetic and how those deep areas of prophetic inspiration are to run.

Amos 3:1-8: *LISTEN TO THIS MESSAGE THAT THE LORD HAS SPOKEN AGAINST YOU, O PEOPLE OF ISRAEL—*

*AGAINST THE ENTIRE FAMILY I RESCUED FROM EGYPT:
"FROM AMONG ALL THE FAMILIES ON THE EARTH, I HAVE
BEEN INTIMATE WITH YOU ALONE. THAT IS WHY I MUST
PUNISH YOU FOR ALL YOUR SINS." CAN TWO PEOPLE
WALK TOGETHER WITHOUT AGREEING ON THE
DIRECTION? DOES A LION EVER ROAR IN A THICKET
WITHOUT FIRST FINDING A VICTIM? DOES A YOUNG LION
GROWL IN ITS DEN WITHOUT FIRST CATCHING ITS PREY?
DOES A BIRD EVER GET CAUGHT IN A TRAP THAT HAS NO
BAIT? DOES A TRAP SPRING SHUT WHEN THERE'S
NOTHING TO CATCH? WHEN THE RAM'S HORN BLOWS A
WARNING, SHOULDN'T THE PEOPLE BE ALARMED? DOES
DISASTER COME TO A CITY UNLESS THE LORD HAS
PLANNED IT? INDEED, THE SOVEREIGN LORD NEVER
DOES ANYTHING UNTIL HE REVEALS HIS PLANS TO HIS
SERVANTS THE PROPHETS. THE LION HAS ROARED—SO
WHO ISN'T FRIGHTENED? THE SOVEREIGN LORD HAS
SPOKEN—SO WHO CAN REFUSE TO PROCLAIM HIS
MESSAGE?*

Amos' proclamation that God does nothing without
first revealing it to the prophets was definitely a
slam on the prophets of his day, who were as
corrupt as many of the prophets we see today. They
claimed to be hearing from God, but they told
people what they wanted to hear for money. By
doing what they did, they were deceiving people,
stealing from them, and only partially giving word
to those who needed it because they were only
doing it for the money. Then they would take what
was given to them from those they exploited and
try to use it as a part of religious ritual in the house
of God.

If they were truly prophets, they should have

known the voice of God and recognized the injustices they were committing. We often think if we are deceiving people or using money in an unjust way that God looks the other way, that it isn't as serious of a matter as something else. We are good at turning our heads to injustice, and we are even better at turning away as perpetrators of injustice through money. Yet using our power or our funds to defraud people or to cheat people out of money is a sin, and it is just as much a sin of injustice as any other sin. God is not indifferent to it. If anything, He is highly attentive to the sins that are committed by those who claim to move in His Name, recognizing them as serious enough to bring down those who follow such behavior.

Amos 4:1-5: *LISTEN TO ME, YOU FAT COWS LIVING IN SAMARIA, YOU WOMEN WHO OPPRESS THE POOR AND CRUSH THE NEEDY, AND WHO ARE ALWAYS CALLING TO YOUR HUSBANDS, "BRING US ANOTHER DRINK!" THE SOVEREIGN LORD HAS SWORN THIS BY HIS HOLINESS: "THE TIME WILL COME WHEN YOU WILL BE LED AWAY WITH HOOKS IN YOUR NOSES. EVERY LAST ONE OF YOU WILL BE DRAGGED AWAY LIKE A FISH ON A HOOK! YOU WILL BE LED OUT THROUGH THE RUINS OF THE WALL; YOU WILL BE THROWN FROM YOUR FORTRESSES," SAYS THE LORD. "GO AHEAD AND OFFER SACRIFICES TO THE IDOLS AT BETHEL. KEEP ON DISOBEYING AT GILGAL. OFFER SACRIFICES EACH MORNING, AND BRING YOUR TITHES EVERY THREE DAYS. PRESENT YOUR BREAD MADE WITH YEAST AS AN OFFERING OF THANKSGIVING. THEN GIVE YOUR EXTRA VOLUNTARY OFFERINGS SO YOU CAN BRAG ABOUT IT EVERYWHERE! THIS IS THE KIND OF THING YOU ISRAELITES LOVE TO DO," SAYS THE SOVEREIGN LORD.*

The book of Amos details how incredibly unattractive unjust money becomes. Even though the people of that era might have lived in a perceived prosperity and comfort, the way they lived was disgraceful. They were not honorable people, living in lazy conditions off the work and exploitation of others. The love of money dominated their lives, their identities, and the way they even treated each other.

Amos 5:1-17: *LISTEN, YOU PEOPLE OF ISRAEL! LISTEN TO THIS FUNERAL SONG I AM SINGING: "THE VIRGIN ISRAEL HAS FALLEN, NEVER TO RISE AGAIN! SHE LIES ABANDONED ON THE GROUND, WITH NO ONE TO HELP HER UP." THE SOVEREIGN LORD SAYS: "WHEN A CITY SENDS A THOUSAND MEN TO BATTLE, ONLY A HUNDRED WILL RETURN. WHEN A TOWN SENDS A HUNDRED, ONLY TEN WILL COME BACK ALIVE." NOW THIS IS WHAT THE LORD SAYS TO THE FAMILY OF ISRAEL: "COME BACK TO ME AND LIVE! DON'T WORSHIP AT THE PAGAN ALTARS AT BETHEL; DON'T GO TO THE SHRINES AT GILGAL OR BEERSHEBA. FOR THE PEOPLE OF GILGAL WILL BE DRAGGED OFF INTO EXILE, AND THE PEOPLE OF BETHEL WILL BE REDUCED TO NOTHING." COME BACK TO THE LORD AND LIVE! OTHERWISE, HE WILL ROAR THROUGH ISRAEL LIKE A FIRE, DEVOURING YOU COMPLETELY. YOUR GODS IN BETHEL WON'T BE ABLE TO QUENCH THE FLAMES. YOU TWIST JUSTICE, MAKING IT A BITTER PILL FOR THE OPPRESSED. YOU TREAT THE RIGHTEOUS LIKE DIRT. IT IS THE LORD WHO CREATED THE STARS, THE PLEIADES AND ORION. HE TURNS DARKNESS INTO MORNING AND DAY INTO NIGHT. HE DRAWS UP WATER FROM THE OCEANS AND POURS IT DOWN AS RAIN ON THE*

LAND. THE LORD IS HIS NAME! WITH BLINDING SPEED AND POWER HE DESTROYS THE STRONG, CRUSHING ALL THEIR DEFENSES. HOW YOU HATE HONEST JUDGES! HOW YOU DESPISE PEOPLE WHO TELL THE TRUTH! YOU TRAMPLE THE POOR, STEALING THEIR GRAIN THROUGH TAXES AND UNFAIR RENT. THEREFORE, THOUGH YOU BUILD BEAUTIFUL STONE HOUSES, YOU WILL NEVER LIVE IN THEM. THOUGH YOU PLANT LUSH VINEYARDS, YOU WILL NEVER DRINK WINE FROM THEM. FOR I KNOW THE VAST NUMBER OF YOUR SINS AND THE DEPTH OF YOUR REBELLIONS. YOU OPPRESS GOOD PEOPLE BY TAKING BRIBES AND DEPRIVE THE POOR OF JUSTICE IN THE COURTS. SO THOSE WHO ARE SMART KEEP THEIR MOUTHS SHUT, FOR IT IS AN EVIL TIME. DO WHAT IS GOOD AND RUN FROM EVIL SO THAT YOU MAY LIVE! THEN THE LORD GOD OF HEAVEN'S ARMIES WILL BE YOUR HELPER, JUST AS YOU HAVE CLAIMED. HATE EVIL AND LOVE WHAT IS GOOD; TURN YOUR COURTS INTO TRUE HALLS OF JUSTICE. PERHAPS EVEN YET THE LORD GOD OF HEAVEN'S ARMIES WILL HAVE MERCY ON THE REMNANT OF HIS PEOPLE. THEREFORE, THIS IS WHAT THE LORD, THE LORD GOD OF HEAVEN'S ARMIES, SAYS: "THERE WILL BE CRYING IN ALL THE PUBLIC SQUARES AND MOURNING IN EVERY STREET. CALL FOR THE FARMERS TO WEEP WITH YOU, AND SUMMON PROFESSIONAL MOURNERS TO WAIL. THERE WILL BE WAILING IN EVERY VINEYARD, FOR I WILL DESTROY THEM ALL," SAYS THE LORD.

Amos proves to us that what we do with our money is just as important as that we do something with it. While yes, it is right to tithe and to give to the Kingdom, it is also right to be just with your money in other ways, as well. We can give all day long to the church with money that was obtained by ill-gotten gain if we don't obey God's precepts in every area of our lives, including our finances. If we don't, we will not see God's blessing upon our lives or our various undertakings. To make a business prosper and a life to prosper, we must be ethical with our finances and fair in our dealings.

MICAH

Micah's general prophetic message was very similar to that of Amos, yet the way he presented it was a little different. He lived in a different time, seeing intense and brutal violence due to warfare that seemingly had no end or answer. Micah's words expressed deep personal lament over the injustices present in Israel, a tone which Amos' prophecy did not have in quite the same way. In terms of rebuke, Micah does call out to the general community of Israelites, but he also pays special attention to rebuke of the leaders, who were leading people astray in some of the worst possible ways.

Micah 3:5-12: *THIS IS WHAT THE LORD SAYS: "YOU FALSE PROPHETS ARE LEADING MY PEOPLE ASTRAY! YOU PROMISE PEACE FOR THOSE WHO GIVE YOU FOOD, BUT YOU DECLARE WAR ON THOSE WHO REFUSE TO FEED YOU. NOW THE NIGHT WILL CLOSE AROUND YOU, CUTTING OFF ALL YOUR VISIONS. DARKNESS WILL COVER YOU, PUTTING AN END TO YOUR PREDICTIONS. THE SUN WILL SET FOR YOU PROPHETS, AND YOUR DAY WILL COME TO AN END. THEN YOU SEERS WILL BE PUT TO SHAME, AND YOU FORTUNE-TELLERS WILL BE DISGRACED. AND YOU*

WILL COVER YOUR FACES BECAUSE THERE IS NO ANSWER FROM GOD." BUT AS FOR ME, I AM FILLED WITH POWER— WITH THE SPIRIT OF THE LORD. I AM FILLED WITH JUSTICE AND STRENGTH TO BOLDLY DECLARE ISRAEL'S SIN AND REBELLION. LISTEN TO ME, YOU LEADERS OF ISRAEL! YOU HATE JUSTICE AND TWIST ALL THAT IS RIGHT. YOU ARE BUILDING JERUSALEM ON A FOUNDATION OF MURDER AND CORRUPTION. YOU RULERS MAKE DECISIONS BASED ON BRIBES; YOU PRIESTS TEACH GOD'S LAWS ONLY FOR A PRICE; YOU PROPHETS WON'T PROPHESY UNLESS YOU ARE PAID. YET ALL OF YOU CLAIM TO DEPEND ON THE LORD. "NO HARM CAN COME TO US," YOU SAY, "FOR THE LORD IS HERE AMONG US." BECAUSE OF YOU, MOUNT ZION WILL BE PLOWED LIKE AN OPEN FIELD; JERUSALEM WILL BE REDUCED TO RUINS! A THICKET WILL GROW ON THE HEIGHTS WHERE THE TEMPLE NOW STANDS.

Even though Micah did not talk about financial corruption as much as Amos did, he still points out the way that financial wrongdoing works hand-in-hand with injustice. If we think the church to be above such corruptions, we need to think again. The prophecy of Micah and Amos alike make it clear that there are people in leadership who use their offices to exploit others for nothing more than a mere profit. This is wrong, no matter who is doing it, or what name they attempt to do it in. As a standard, we need to raise the bar so our leaders remain financially accountable.

HABAKKUK

Unlike Amos and Micah, the book of Habakkuk is a

dialogue between the Prophet Habakkuk and God Himself. The main theme of Habakkuk's inquiries and discussion with God relates to human evil, and the answer for such when it seems like one is surrounded by evil at every pass.

In Habakkuk's questions about evil include issues of financial abuses, with those who are abominable with their wealth, exploiting others and taking advantage of them through it.

Habakkuk 2:1-14: *"WRITE MY ANSWER PLAINLY ON TABLETS, SO THAT A RUNNER CAN CARRY THE CORRECT MESSAGE TO OTHERS. THIS VISION IS FOR A FUTURE TIME. IT DESCRIBES THE END, AND IT WILL BE FULFILLED. IF IT SEEMS SLOW IN COMING, WAIT PATIENTLY, FOR IT WILL SURELY TAKE PLACE. IT WILL NOT BE DELAYED. "LOOK AT THE PROUD! THEY TRUST IN THEMSELVES, AND THEIR LIVES ARE CROOKED. BUT THE RIGHTEOUS WILL LIVE BY THEIR FAITHFULNESS TO GOD. WEALTH IS TREACHEROUS, AND THE ARROGANT ARE NEVER AT REST. THEY OPEN THEIR MOUTHS AS WIDE AS THE GRAVE, AND LIKE DEATH, THEY ARE NEVER SATISFIED. IN THEIR GREED THEY HAVE GATHERED UP MANY NATIONS AND SWALLOWED MANY PEOPLES. "BUT SOON THEIR CAPTIVES WILL TAUNT THEM. THEY WILL MOCK THEM, SAYING, 'WHAT SORROW AWAITS YOU THIEVES! NOW YOU WILL GET WHAT YOU DESERVE! YOU'VE BECOME RICH BY EXTORTION, BUT HOW MUCH LONGER CAN THIS GO ON?' SUDDENLY, YOUR DEBTORS WILL TAKE ACTION. THEY WILL TURN ON YOU AND TAKE ALL YOU HAVE, WHILE YOU STAND TREMBLING AND HELPLESS. BECAUSE YOU HAVE PLUNDERED MANY NATIONS, NOW ALL THE SURVIVORS WILL PLUNDER YOU. YOU COMMITTED MURDER THROUGHOUT THE COUNTRYSIDE AND FILLED*

THE TOWNS WITH VIOLENCE. "WHAT SORROW AWAITS YOU WHO BUILD BIG HOUSES WITH MONEY GAINED DISHONESTLY! YOU BELIEVE YOUR WEALTH WILL BUY SECURITY, PUTTING YOUR FAMILY'S NEST BEYOND THE REACH OF DANGER. BUT BY THE MURDERS YOU COMMITTED, YOU HAVE SHAMED YOUR NAME AND FORFEITED YOUR LIVES. THE VERY STONES IN THE WALLS CRY OUT AGAINST YOU, AND THE BEAMS IN THE CEILINGS ECHO THE COMPLAINT. "WHAT SORROW AWAITS YOU WHO BUILD CITIES WITH MONEY GAINED THROUGH MURDER AND CORRUPTION! HAS NOT THE LORD OF HEAVEN'S ARMIES PROMISED THAT THE WEALTH OF NATIONS WILL TURN TO ASHES? THEY WORK SO HARD, BUT ALL IN VAIN! FOR AS THE WATERS FILL THE SEA, THE EARTH WILL BE FILLED WITH AN AWARENESS OF THE GLORY OF THE LORD.

Habakkuk's prophecy foresaw the destruction of those who relied on riches (and in the process, the exploitation and evil of others) rather than living by faith in God. None of the prophets ignored the fact that it takes money to live, and Habakkuk was not doing this either, not in the least. The problem emerged when people were living by their greed rather than their faith, and that when they reach a point where greed controls their lives, they lose what they have.

If we build upon greed, love of money, and the things of the evil in the world, we will see ourselves fall when those things fall. When it comes to money, we must be very careful to plant properly and spend our finances in a proper way.

HAGGAI

The prophet Haggai was, like Amos, probably not real popular in his day. Haggai lived in a reconstruction period following exile, in which Israel had returned from captivity. After sixteen years, the Israelites were living in their own comforts: they had nice houses, they had replaced what they'd lost during their years of captivity, but the temple of God laid in ruins. Despite so many years of opportunities to rebuild the spiritual ministry, Israel ignored this opportunity and built themselves up, personally, instead.

Haggai 1:1-15: *ON AUGUST 29 OF THE SECOND YEAR OF KING DARIUS'S REIGN, THE LORD GAVE A MESSAGE THROUGH THE PROPHET HAGGAI TO ZERUBBABEL SON OF SHEALTIEL, GOVERNOR OF JUDAH, AND TO JESHUA SON OF JEHOZADAK, THE HIGH PRIEST. "THIS IS WHAT THE LORD OF HEAVEN'S ARMIES SAYS: THE PEOPLE ARE SAYING, 'THE TIME HAS NOT YET COME TO REBUILD THE HOUSE OF THE LORD.'" THEN THE LORD SENT THIS MESSAGE THROUGH THE PROPHET HAGGAI: "WHY ARE YOU LIVING IN LUXURIOUS HOUSES WHILE MY HOUSE LIES IN RUINS? THIS IS WHAT THE LORD OF HEAVEN'S ARMIES SAYS: LOOK AT WHAT'S HAPPENING TO YOU! YOU HAVE PLANTED MUCH BUT HARVEST LITTLE. YOU EAT BUT ARE NOT SATISFIED. YOU DRINK BUT ARE STILL THIRSTY. YOU PUT ON CLOTHES BUT CANNOT KEEP WARM. YOUR WAGES DISAPPEAR AS THOUGH YOU WERE PUTTING THEM IN POCKETS FILLED WITH HOLES! "THIS IS WHAT THE LORD OF HEAVEN'S ARMIES SAYS: LOOK AT WHAT'S HAPPENING TO YOU! NOW GO UP INTO THE HILLS, BRING DOWN TIMBER, AND REBUILD MY HOUSE.*

THEN I WILL TAKE PLEASURE IN IT AND BE HONORED, SAYS THE LORD. YOU HOPED FOR RICH HARVESTS, BUT THEY WERE POOR. AND WHEN YOU BROUGHT YOUR HARVEST HOME, I BLEW IT AWAY. WHY? BECAUSE MY HOUSE LIES IN RUINS, SAYS THE LORD OF HEAVEN'S ARMIES, WHILE ALL OF YOU ARE BUSY BUILDING YOUR OWN FINE HOUSES. IT'S BECAUSE OF YOU THAT THE HEAVENS WITHHOLD THE DEW AND THE EARTH PRODUCES NO CROPS. I HAVE CALLED FOR A DROUGHT ON YOUR FIELDS AND HILLS—A DROUGHT TO WITHER THE GRAIN AND GRAPES AND OLIVE TREES AND ALL YOUR OTHER CROPS, A DROUGHT TO STARVE YOU AND YOUR LIVESTOCK AND TO RUIN EVERYTHING YOU HAVE WORKED SO HARD TO GET." THEN ZERUBBABEL SON OF SHEALTIEL, AND JESHUA SON OF JEHOZADAK, THE HIGH PRIEST, AND THE WHOLE REMNANT OF GOD'S PEOPLE BEGAN TO OBEY THE MESSAGE FROM THE LORD THEIR GOD. WHEN THEY HEARD THE WORDS OF THE PROPHET HAGGAI, WHOM THE LORD THEIR GOD HAD SENT, THE PEOPLE FEARED THE LORD. THEN HAGGAI, THE LORD'S MESSENGER, GAVE THE PEOPLE THIS MESSAGE FROM THE LORD: "I AM WITH YOU, SAYS THE LORD!" SO THE LORD SPARKED THE ENTHUSIASM OF ZERUBBABEL SON OF SHEALTIEL, GOVERNOR OF JUDAH, AND THE ENTHUSIASM OF JESHUA SON OF JEHOZADAK, THE HIGH PRIEST, AND THE ENTHUSIASM OF THE WHOLE REMNANT OF GOD'S PEOPLE. THEY BEGAN TO WORK ON THE HOUSE OF THEIR GOD, THE LORD OF HEAVEN'S ARMIES, ON SEPTEMBER 21 OF THE SECOND YEAR OF KING DARIUS'S REIGN.

In contrast to Amos where the Israelites were comfortable and giving with money that was stolen or acquired through less-than-honorable means, in

Haggai, they were just not giving, at all. Instead of giving to God, they were withholding funds for themselves, pursuing their own needs, wants, and desires while ignoring God's clear command to ensure that His Kingdom continue throughout the generations. The Israelites were given clear examples of the ways that God was speaking to them about their lack of financial disciplines in the ministry. Even though they were pursuing for themselves and they'd achieved a certain level of personal comfort, they were still experiencing the futility of working hard and not seeing the full results of their labors. God was crying out to them in their lack, in their futility, in natural disasters, and in their own ruin, to get them to examine the ruins of the ministry and the need for the ministry to be rebuilt and reestablished.

The result was Zerubbabel, a leader, Joshua son of Jozadak, the high priest, and the people of Israel's commitment to get the temple rebuilt and the work of God to go forward. This required every Israelite to resume their financial giving to the ministry and to move forward with the project.

Haggai 2:1-9: *THEN ON OCTOBER 17 OF THAT SAME YEAR, THE LORD SENT ANOTHER MESSAGE THROUGH THE PROPHET HAGGAI. "SAY THIS TO ZERUBBABEL SON OF SHEALTIEL, GOVERNOR OF JUDAH, AND TO JESHUA SON OF JEHOZADAK, THE HIGH PRIEST, AND TO THE REMNANT OF GOD'S PEOPLE THERE IN THE LAND: 'DOES ANYONE REMEMBER THIS HOUSE—THIS TEMPLE—IN ITS FORMER SPLENDOR? HOW, IN COMPARISON, DOES IT LOOK TO YOU NOW? IT MUST SEEM LIKE NOTHING AT ALL! BUT NOW THE LORD SAYS: BE STRONG, ZERUBBABEL. BE*

STRONG, JESHUA SON OF JEHOZADAK, THE HIGH PRIEST. BE STRONG, ALL YOU PEOPLE STILL LEFT IN THE LAND. AND NOW GET TO WORK, FOR I AM WITH YOU, SAYS THE LORD OF HEAVEN'S ARMIES. MY SPIRIT REMAINS AMONG YOU, JUST AS I PROMISED WHEN YOU CAME OUT OF EGYPT. SO DO NOT BE AFRAID.' "FOR THIS IS WHAT THE LORD OF HEAVEN'S ARMIES SAYS: IN JUST A LITTLE WHILE I WILL AGAIN SHAKE THE HEAVENS AND THE EARTH, THE OCEANS AND THE DRY LAND. I WILL SHAKE ALL THE NATIONS, AND THE TREASURES OF ALL THE NATIONS WILL BE BROUGHT TO THIS TEMPLE. I WILL FILL THIS PLACE WITH GLORY, SAYS THE LORD OF HEAVEN'S ARMIES. THE SILVER IS MINE, AND THE GOLD IS MINE, SAYS THE LORD OF HEAVEN'S ARMIES. THE FUTURE GLORY OF THIS TEMPLE WILL BE GREATER THAN ITS PAST GLORY, SAYS THE LORD OF HEAVEN'S ARMIES. AND IN THIS PLACE I WILL BRING PEACE. I, THE LORD OF HEAVEN'S ARMIES, HAVE SPOKEN!"

The book of Haggai, as short as it is, challenges the believer in their giving to the Lord, even when it might seem like personal priorities are more important than ministry expansions. In Haggai, the Israelites had lived in captivity and then returned, which we all know means that they had rebuilding their own lives on their minds. Their focus was restoring what they lost, rather than looking at the spiritual losses in play and making sure their worship and their spiritual needs were regained. Too often, we want to put ourselves ahead of God in church. We hear about healing and about the enemy restoring what was lost, but we don't hear the right way to go about those things. If the people of Israel had been following God's precepts for giving, they wouldn't have been in lack. They would have trusted Him to recognize that in giving, they still had plenty left to prosper as individuals and live in the security and comfort they desired.

If the silver and gold belong to God, all that we rely on in this world for our currency and our life sustainment, then we must be sure to put God first with our "silver and gold" (money). If we are willing to put God first with the form of our lives that we consider to be the fluid force allowing us to live, then we will be willing to put God first in every other area, as well. If we allow the silver and gold to hold us back, then we don't recognize where it came from, and we aren't honoring God with our lives as we claim to be. As I stated earlier, what we do with our money is a dead giveaway as to where God is in our lives and how much of a priority He is, or is not.

We often put ourselves in position to compete with God and God's work without stepping back and realizing that doing such puts our own needs and wants ahead of God and displays no trust or faith in the work that God does in our lives. We tell God we want increase, but then we don't trust Him enough to bring that increase to us by maintaining our finances according to His precepts. Haggai shows us that if we want to be a truly blessed people, we need to make sure that our souls and spirits prosper. We can't do this if we don't cough up our money and give as God has commanded us to do so. Until we are willing to play by God's financial rules, we are going to live in futility and lack.

MALACHI

Malachi's prophecy differs from those of Amos, Micah, Habakkuk, and Haggai in who it was directed towards. The prophet Malachi lived in a time of widespread corruption among the priests, the spiritual leaders, of Israel. Unlike in Haggai where the problem was most definitely the people and in Amos where the problem was both the people and the leaders, Malachi gives a stern rebuking to leaders who kept back the best part of the sacrifices for themselves and then claimed they didn't understand why God was reprimanding them and refusing to bless the work of their hands. There were many things the leaders were doing wrong, but one of the primary ones related to tithes and offerings, a passage of Scripture often invoked during offering times at churches today. One way the leaders were disobeying God was by stealing and misappropriating tithes and offerings.

Malachi 3:6-12: *"I AM THE LORD, AND I DO NOT CHANGE. THAT IS WHY YOU DESCENDANTS OF JACOB ARE NOT ALREADY DESTROYED. EVER SINCE THE DAYS OF YOUR ANCESTORS, YOU HAVE SCORNED MY DECREES AND FAILED TO OBEY THEM. NOW RETURN TO ME, AND I WILL RETURN TO YOU," SAYS THE LORD OF HEAVEN'S ARMIES. "BUT YOU ASK, 'HOW CAN WE RETURN WHEN WE HAVE NEVER GONE AWAY?' "SHOULD PEOPLE CHEAT GOD? YET YOU HAVE CHEATED ME! "BUT YOU ASK, 'WHAT DO YOU MEAN? WHEN DID WE EVER CHEAT YOU?' "YOU HAVE CHEATED ME OF THE TITHES AND OFFERINGS DUE TO ME. YOU ARE UNDER A CURSE, FOR YOUR WHOLE NATION HAS BEEN CHEATING ME. BRING ALL THE TITHES*

INTO THE STOREHOUSE SO THERE WILL BE ENOUGH FOOD IN MY TEMPLE. IF YOU DO," SAYS THE LORD OF HEAVEN'S ARMIES, "I WILL OPEN THE WINDOWS OF HEAVEN FOR YOU. I WILL POUR OUT A BLESSING SO GREAT YOU WON'T HAVE ENOUGH ROOM TO TAKE IT IN! TRY IT! PUT ME TO THE TEST! YOUR CROPS WILL BE ABUNDANT, FOR I WILL GUARD THEM FROM INSECTS AND DISEASE. YOUR GRAPES WILL NOT FALL FROM THE VINE BEFORE THEY ARE RIPE," SAYS THE LORD OF HEAVEN'S ARMIES. "THEN ALL NATIONS WILL CALL YOU BLESSED, FOR YOUR LAND WILL BE SUCH A DELIGHT," SAYS THE LORD OF HEAVEN'S ARMIES.

When we often quote this passage, we use it to tell people not to rob God by refusing to tithe. I won't say this can't apply at all, because it is very possible that seeing the abuses of the day, people withheld tithes because they distrusted their leaders. We see this in people today, who try to make it seem as if refusing to offer anywhere, to any leader, is better than finding a suitable ministry to sit under and tithe through. This isn't the direct context of the passage, however, because Malachi's words were to the leaders who were abusing God's system. It was the priests who were told to bring all the tithes into the storehouse, to watch God rain down upon the entire nation of Israel and bring forth blessings that the leaders and the people sought to discover.

Malachi teaches us that greed is not an attribute exclusive to any one type of person. Just because someone is called into ministry doesn't make them immune to greed or the temptation to avoid God's precepts in a fit of spiritual distrust.

The temptations of greed come upon the great and the small alike, and hits those in ministry as well as those who have never graced a pulpit. When a leader goes before God, they need to make sure they are not robbing God by aimlessly stealing from His people and calling it their own. Leaders, as well as members, must check themselves and their commitment before God, and avoid the temptation to use finances in a fleshly manner.

LEARNING FROM THE PROPHETS ABOUT MONEY

We have learned from the writings of these minor prophets about money a few key things.

1. **Greed is not exclusive to one "type" of person.** – We tend to assign stereotypes when it comes to greed, thinking ministers can't be greedy, so-called "holy" people can't be greedy, even that rich people can't be greedy, because they already have enough money. Greed can hit anyone, anywhere, at any time, because of how they feel about and regard having money.

2. **If we put our confidence in money, we will not be able to stand before God.** – If we talk about living by faith, that means we live by faith, not money. It sounds obvious, but it also means that we don't spend so much time focusing on getting money through our faith. It means we trust God and do our best.

3. **If the silver and gold belong to God, then what we do with our money shows where God is in our lives.** – A simple principle we have already spoken on.

4. **Living by money equates to wickedness.** – If your whole life is spent in pursuit of money, then your life is wrapped up in the love of money.

JOURNALING

- What does the Prophet Amos teach us about money and injustice?
- What does the Prophet Micah teach us about the way that financial corruption works with moral injustice?
- How does the Prophet Habakkuk discuss money in connection with those who do evil?
- What does the Prophet Haggai teach us about giving and the Kingdom, especially in restoration periods?
- What does the Prophet Malachi teach us about finances and leadership?

7 Understanding Ministry Finances

EVEN though we talk about finances in church, very few people understand the complications of ministry finances and the legalities that ministers must go through in order to maintain their ministries. Yes, ministers need money to keep their work operational, but they also have to follow strict policies and procedures that relate to financial accountability and inability to maintain personal profits from the monies donated.

Understanding the way that ministry finances operate helps all of us in a few ways. The first way is that it helps us to recognize how difficult it is to maintain a ministry from a financial perspective. We like to talk about ministry from the perspective of what an honor it is to be called and how awesome it is to do the work of God, but we don't often consider the nitty-gritty details that ministers encounter on a regular basis. Financial complications is definitely one of them, and gaining an appreciation for what a minister goes through financially to maintain ministry helps those who are a part of that ministry appreciate the work in a deeper way. The second way is that it helps us to see the protections put in place in order to weed out scammers and false ministers from true ones. The third way is if a ministry's finances are properly structured, you can know the difference your giving makes through the different communications provided by the ministry at hand.

No matter what your relationship to ministry: whether you are in it yourself or you attend a ministry or follow one, you are in a position to benefit from the information present in this chapter. As much as possible, I will be simplifying the different angles of finances present in a ministry and making it so you understand why giving is important and foolproof for those who are a part of the work of God in this present form.

CUTTING THROUGH THE EXCUSES OF WHY PEOPLE DON'T GIVE

Let's start by cutting through the different excuses people offer for refusing to give to a ministry:

- I had a bad experience somewhere else.
- I can't afford it.
- I have kids.
- I've been church hurt.
- All ministers are crooks.
- All televangelists steal people's money.
- I can't tell a true minister from a false one.

As one who has been in ministry for nearly twenty years, I have heard all these excuses, more than once, time and time again. It's ironic that nobody comes up with new excuses, but keeps repeating the same ones over and over again. This means that the excuses are…well…BORING.

If you call yourself a Christian, than giving should be a part of your nature. There is no "I can't afford it" for any variety of reasons that you come up with. Likewise, not all ministers are crooks, not all ministers on television steal people's money, and it is really unfair to stigmatize all leaders in that same manner. There are plenty of dishonest, disrespectable people in all professions, but we don't see people running around saying they are going to stop going to the store or stop buying things online or stop calling a lawyer when they get in legal trouble. There are people who disgrace these industries, as well, but we don't stop shelling out our money for their products. The excuses as pertain to ministry and ministers falter, plain and simple, and reveals hearts that just don't want to give and seek to find excuses to refrain from giving.

Philippians 2:13: *FOR GOD IS WORKING IN YOU, GIVING YOU THE DESIRE AND THE POWER TO DO WHAT PLEASES HIM.*

We should be excited about giving because it gives us a tangible, hands-on opportunity to stand up and be counted within a ministry setting. It lets the product of our income become a part of that work, thus we all have a stake and a part in whatever God is doing through that ministry. It should be our privilege to honor God with our finances through our giving, at all times and in all seasons. Non-profit organizations operate on the donation principle, because they are regarded as organizations of public interest. This means that even though we tend to encourage churches and ministries to rely on grants for their project funding, the majority of money that comes into a church or ministry will come via donation form. It is, therefore, all the more important that we grow out of the negative attitudes we have about giving and get in there to support our Kingdom-based organizations all the more.

A RUN-DOWN OF NON-PROFIT GUIDELINES

In order to understand the way that ministries function financially, it's important to understand the basics of non-profit guidelines and how non-profit corporations work. While some guidelines do vary between countries, there are certain basic principles that apply to non-profit governance and financial accountability.

In my book, *About My Father's Business: Professional Ministry for Kingdom Leaders*, I devote an entire chapter to 501(c)(3) status and the ins and outs of it. I am not going to do that in-depth here in this book, so if you would like a more thorough explanation on it, feel free to check it out. At the heart of 501(c)(3) status is the reality that if we are to be blameless in our ministerial conducts, that includes our finances. As non-profit organizations, the government requires us to be accountable in our practices, lacking nothing and standing fully accountable before the people that we serve in our work.

Daniel 6:4: *THEN THE OTHER ADMINISTRATORS AND HIGH OFFICERS BEGAN SEARCHING FOR SOME FAULT IN THE WAY DANIEL WAS HANDLING GOVERNMENT AFFAIRS, BUT THEY COULDN'T FIND ANYTHING TO CRITICIZE OR CONDEMN. HE WAS FAITHFUL, ALWAYS RESPONSIBLE, AND COMPLETELY TRUSTWORTHY.*

In order to understand non-profit status, we need to first recognize that being non-profit renders an organization exempt from the 30% federal income tax rate required of for-profit corporations. Being non-profit means the purpose of the organization has no personal profit for any of the partners in the organization. This means its primary purpose does not exist to make the board members or primary members of an organization wealthy. This does not prohibit non-profit organizations from paying their executives or staff, but it does prevent them from capitalizing on funds for personal purposes, such as taking an unreasonably high salary from the organization. Tax exempt organizations must keep careful records of earnings and be clear to separate personal earnings from those that are raised by the non-profit organization for charitable purposes.

There are all sorts of non-profit organizations, including schools, hospitals, ministries, religious groups, literary groups, civic organizations, public safety groups, sports groups, anti-abuse organizations, advocacy groups that work to stop prejudice or that uphold civil rights, organizations against community deterioration and juvenile delinquency, scientific endeavors, and charities. The base purpose of every single non-profit is the betterment of humanity through the means of their ideals and beliefs, which they seek to present in action form through a non-profit organization. The purpose, mission, and vision of an organization must be clear, articulated through documentation, and presented to the appropriate agencies for approval.

Romans 13:1: *EVERYONE MUST SUBMIT TO GOVERNING AUTHORITIES. FOR ALL AUTHORITY COMES FROM GOD, AND THOSE IN POSITIONS OF AUTHORITY HAVE BEEN PLACED THERE BY GOD.*

Being legally recognized as a non-profit organization is not a right, but a privilege extended to an organization by the government to agencies that meet the necessary criteria. This means that as it is not a right, it can be removed at any time if an organization is found to be in non-compliance with federal statutes. As a result, there are those who debate the validity of 501(c)(3) status and applying for such under the federal government. We like the idea of accountability, but we don't like the idea of requirements for such under governmental watch. The reality is that non-profit status makes it much harder for charlatans to run off with hard-earned money that should be used for charitable purposes, and the holdings, reportings, and bookkeeping of an organization are subject to public inspection at any time upon request. Holding non-profit status gives legitimacy to an organization, it is easier to receive donations, and you can apply for grants, all of which cannot be obtained without that status.

An organization should file for non-profit status as soon as the question of donations and funding starts to arise. Most professionals suggest a filing should occur when an organization has somewhere around twenty-five to fifty members, if not sooner. Whenever there is a need for increased donations, regular money is coming into an organization, or there is a need for outside funding, non-profit status becomes a requirement.

THE MINISTRY BOARD

In order to maintain tax-exempt status, all churches and ministries must have a board of directors in place. The purpose of a board of directors is to balance out the ideals of an organization and ensure that financial and business decisions are not for any one individual's personal benefit. In a church setting, the board of directors is usually made up of church elders. In a ministry setting, it usually consists of individuals who assist in ministry, in a bishopric capacity, or other leaders who are close with the connection of the international, national, or governing body of the organization.

Acts 15:1-11: *WHILE PAUL AND BARNABAS WERE AT ANTIOCH OF SYRIA, SOME MEN FROM JUDEA ARRIVED AND BEGAN TO TEACH THE BELIEVERS: "UNLESS YOU ARE CIRCUMCISED AS REQUIRED BY THE LAW OF MOSES, YOU CANNOT BE SAVED." PAUL AND BARNABAS DISAGREED WITH THEM, ARGUING VEHEMENTLY. FINALLY, THE*

CHURCH DECIDED TO SEND PAUL AND BARNABAS TO JERUSALEM, ACCOMPANIED BY SOME LOCAL BELIEVERS, TO TALK TO THE APOSTLES AND ELDERS ABOUT THIS QUESTION. THE CHURCH SENT THE DELEGATES TO JERUSALEM, AND THEY STOPPED ALONG THE WAY IN PHOENICIA AND SAMARIA TO VISIT THE BELIEVERS. THEY TOLD THEM—MUCH TO EVERYONE'S JOY—THAT THE GENTILES, TOO, WERE BEING CONVERTED. WHEN THEY ARRIVED IN JERUSALEM, BARNABAS AND PAUL WERE WELCOMED BY THE WHOLE CHURCH, INCLUDING THE APOSTLES AND ELDERS. THEY REPORTED EVERYTHING GOD HAD DONE THROUGH THEM. BUT THEN SOME OF THE BELIEVERS WHO BELONGED TO THE SECT OF THE PHARISEES STOOD UP AND INSISTED, "THE GENTILE CONVERTS MUST BE CIRCUMCISED AND REQUIRED TO FOLLOW THE LAW OF MOSES." SO THE APOSTLES AND ELDERS MET TOGETHER TO RESOLVE THIS ISSUE. AT THE MEETING, AFTER A LONG DISCUSSION, PETER STOOD AND ADDRESSED THEM AS FOLLOWS: "BROTHERS, YOU ALL KNOW THAT GOD CHOSE ME FROM AMONG YOU SOME TIME AGO TO PREACH TO THE GENTILES SO THAT THEY COULD HEAR THE GOOD NEWS AND BELIEVE. GOD KNOWS PEOPLE'S HEARTS, AND HE CONFIRMED THAT HE ACCEPTS GENTILES BY GIVING THEM THE HOLY SPIRIT, JUST AS HE DID TO US. HE MADE NO DISTINCTION BETWEEN US AND THEM, FOR HE CLEANSED THEIR HEARTS THROUGH FAITH. SO WHY ARE YOU NOW CHALLENGING GOD BY BURDENING THE GENTILE BELIEVERS WITH A YOKE THAT NEITHER WE NOR OUR ANCESTORS WERE ABLE TO BEAR? WE BELIEVE THAT WE ARE ALL SAVED THE SAME WAY, BY THE UNDESERVED GRACE OF THE LORD JESUS."

Board meetings are held as often as determined by

the organization, and feature agendas, new projects, and other items that go before the governing board. Even though board members typically share the beliefs and ideals of the organization, that doesn't mean everyone always agrees on the best way to handle things or get things done. Board members are not related to the founder of an organization (or are not supposed to be), and that means that the positions sometimes change or rotate, for different reasons. The founder of an organization is typically the president, with other members installed into different positions.

YEARLY REPORTING

Tax-exempt organizations are required to report annually to the IRS using specific forms as to the financial amount of donations that have been received by that organization within a twelve-month period of time. Some states also require non-profits to report to a state organization, as well.

1 Corinthians 4:2: *NOW, A PERSON WHO IS PUT IN CHARGE AS A MANAGER MUST BE FAITHFUL.*

In compliance with annual compliances for public inspection, many ministries also maintain annual reports (some fancy, some simple) to show the way that donations have contributed toward the different goals and activities of an organization.

MINISTRY PARTNERSHIP

Someone would probably ask what this is doing

here since I already mentioned ministries as a part of tithing and offerings earlier. This book is filled with lots of information about His principles for your finances, and part of that information is about ministry partnership. So yes, this section of this book serves to examine ministry partnership and the role you play in it. In paralleling what I spoke of earlier, a lot of people accuse ministers of being money-grubbing and solicitous when it comes to funds and although I am beyond positive that some are, I'm not one of them, and I know many ministers who do not fall into that category, either. If most of us were in this job for the money, we would have left it a long time ago. Thus, the reason we need to discuss ministry partnership? Now that you have a general idea of how ministry finances work, it's important to put those principles into action.

Mark 16:15: *GO YE INTO ALL THE WORLD, AND PREACH THE GOSPEL TO EVERY CREATURE.* (KJV)

Mark 16:15 isn't a passage we would typically associate with ministry partnership, but it has relevance in more ways than we can imagine. Naturally we are all called to "preach the Gospel" and witness to the truth, every one of us, every day, through the calling God has placed on our lives. But there are people whose calling in life is to literally preach and evangelize through ministries and to bring the Gospel to every creature through their work. When Jesus made the proclamation to go into the world, He was speaking to those who would become the first ministers, the first apostles of the early church. As early as New Testament times, support for ministries has been recognized as an important and blessed aspect of giving, not to be overlooked or rejected. The Apostle Paul spoke in thanks of his ministry partners and contributors. Jesus and His apostles had a treasury, which seems to suggest they did receive donations and offerings from people. Giving financially to ministries is not a new idea made up by televangelists and is an imperative part of the Christian life and continuing in the proclamation of the Gospel.

Philippians 1:7,11, 15-21, 25-30: *EVEN AS IT IS MEET FOR ME TO THINK THIS OF YOU ALL, BECAUSE I HAVE YOU IN MY HEART; INASMUCH AS BOTH IN MY BONDS, AND IN THE DEFENCE AND CONFIRMATION OF THE GOSPEL, YE ALL ARE PARTAKERS OF MY GRACE...BEING FILLED WITH THE FRUITS OF RIGHTEOUSNESS, WHICH ARE BY JESUS CHRIST, UNTO THE GLORY AND PRAISE OF GOD...SOME INDEED PREACH CHRIST EVEN OF ENVY AND STRIFE; AND SOME ALSO OF GOOD WILL: THE ONE PREACH CHRIST OF CONTENTION, NOT SINCERELY, SUPPOSING TO ADD AFFLICTION TO MY BONDS: BUT THE OTHER OF LOVE, KNOWING THAT I AM SET FOR THE DEFENSE OF THE GOSPEL. WHAT THEN? NOTWITHSTANDING, EVERY WAY, WHETHER IN PRETENCE OR IN TRUTH, CHRIST IS PREACHED; AND I THEREIN DO REJOICE, YEA, AND WILL REJOICE. FOR I KNOW THAT THIS SHALL TURN TO MY SALVATION THROUGH YOUR PRAYER, AND THE SUPPLY OF THE SPIRIT OF JESUS CHRIST, ACCORDING TO MY EARNEST EXPECTATION AND MY HOPE, THAT IN NOTHING I SHALL BE ASHAMED, BUT THAT WITH ALL BOLDNESS, AS ALWAYS, SO NOW ALSO CHRIST SHALL BE MAGNIFIED IN*

MY BODY, WHETHER IT BE BY LIFE, OR BY DEATH. AND HAVING THIS CONFIDENCE, I KNOW THAT I SHALL ABIDE AND CONTINUE WITH YOU ALL FOR YOUR FURTHERANCE AND JOY OF FAITH; THAT YOUR REJOICING MAY BE MORE ABUNDANT IN JESUS CHRIST FOR ME BY MY COMING TO YOU AGAIN...ONLY LET YOUR CONVERSATION BE AS IT BECOMETH THE GOSPEL OF CHRIST: THAT WHETHER I COME AND SEE YOU, OR ELSE BE ABSENT, I MAY HEAR OF YOUR AFFAIRS, THAT YE STAND FAST IN ONE SPIRIT, WITH ONE MIND STRIVING TOGETHER FOR THE FAITH OF THE GOSPEL; AND IN NOTHING TERRIFIED BY YOUR ADVERSARIES: WHICH IS TO THEM AN EVIDENT TOKEN OF PERDITION, BUT TO YOU OF SALVATION, AND THAT OF GOD. FOR UNTO YOU IT IS GIVEN IN THE BEHALF OF CHRIST, NOT ONLY TO BELIEVE ON HIM, BUT ALSO TO SUFFER FOR HIS SAKE; HAVING THE SAME CONFLICT WHICH YE SAW IN ME, AND NOW HEAR TO BE IN ME. (KJV)

Matthew 10:41-42: *IF YOU RECEIVE A PROPHET AS ONE WHO SPEAKS FOR GOD, YOU WILL BE GIVEN THE SAME REWARD AS A PROPHET. AND IF YOU RECEIVE RIGHTEOUS PEOPLE BECAUSE OF THEIR RIGHTEOUSNESS, YOU WILL BE GIVEN A REWARD LIKE THEIRS. AND IF YOU GIVE EVEN A CUP OF COLD WATER TO ONE OF THE LEAST OF MY FOLLOWERS, YOU WILL SURELY BE REWARDED.*

These passages both parallel an important truth about ministry participation: those who contribute to the ministry partake in and receive the grace of that ministry's anointing, too. The results of financial giving to a ministry are visible in advance of the Gospel, are visible within your own life, and are visible in the quality of the ministry. Giving does make a difference, it is not without relevance, and it does qualify an individual to have a participation in the work, whether they are able to physically go into the world themselves, or not.

Philippians 4:3-7 and 14-17: *AND I INTREAT THEE ALSO, TRUE YOKEFELLOW, HELP THOSE WOMEN WHICH LABOURED WITH ME IN THE GOSPEL, WITH CLEMENT ALSO, AND WITH OTHER MY FELLOW LABOURERS, WHOSE NAMES ARE IN THE BOOK OF LIFE. REJOICE IN THE LORD ALWAYS: AND AGAIN I SAY, REJOICE. LET YOUR MODERATION BE KNOWN UNTO ALL MEN. THE LORD IS AT HAND. BE CAREFUL FOR NOTHING; BUT IN EVERY THING BY PRAYER AND SUPPLICATION WITH THANKSGIVING LET YOUR REQUESTS BE MADE KNOWN UNTO GOD. AND THE PEACE OF GOD, WHICH PASSETH ALL UNDERSTANDING, SHALL KEEP YOUR HEARTS AND MINDS THROUGH CHRIST JESUS...NOTWITHSTANDING YE HAVE WELL DONE, THAT YE DID COMMUNICATE WITH MY AFFLICTION. NOW YE PHILIPPIANS KNOW ALSO, THAT IN THE BEGINNING OF THE GOSPEL, WHEN I DEPARTED FROM MACEDONIA, NO CHURCH COMMUNICATED WITH ME AS CONCERNING GIVING AND RECEIVING, BUT YE ONLY. FOR EVEN IN THESSALONICA YE SENT ONCE AND AGAIN UNTO MY NECESSITY. NOT BECAUSE I DESIRE A GIFT: BUT I DESIRE FRUIT THAT MAY ABOUND TO YOUR ACCOUNT.* (KJV)

Those who give to ministries partake in the reward of the fruitage of ministries, because in the need of the ministry they partake of the difficulty enough to be supportive. This is why ministry partnership is so important, so vital and so transforming to both involved in the relationship. Committed, regular giving in tithes, offerings, and participation make the lasting difference for the ministry you commit to work with financially.

THINGS THAT MINISTERS NEED TO CONSIDER IN MINISTRY FINANCES

There are certain principles that apply to all financial circumstances, no matter who is involved in their execution. As a final point of examination in this chapter, there are a few additional things that we need to recognize and consider both in our giving and our work of the ministry.

The major thing we need to recognize in ministry is that we need to be positioned to grow our ministries. We often talk about wanting to grow our ministries or about having large ministries, but when it comes down to the realities of ministry, we don't set ourselves up for success. We hope God will take care of all the needs and issues we will encounter, and we don't set our sights on the realities that aspire for financial success. This has led to the stunted growth and downfall of many ministries, not to mention a complete and total stagnation in many others.

Too often we attribute God's will to the lack of a ministry's growth when it often has nothing to do with a ministry's quality or purpose. Sometimes ministers, seeking spiritual things more than natural ones, don't realize that our actions in the natural also effect the development of our ministries. As a rule, ministry isn't all spiritual; it is also a business, and requires business judgment and business decisions.

Proverbs 15:22: *PLANS GO WRONG FOR LACK OF ADVICE; MANY ADVISERS BRING SUCCESS.*

Luke 14:28-30: *BUT DON'T BEGIN UNTIL YOU COUNT THE COST. FOR WHO WOULD BEGIN CONSTRUCTION OF A BUILDING WITHOUT FIRST CALCULATING THE COST TO SEE IF THERE IS ENOUGH MONEY TO FINISH IT? OTHERWISE, YOU MIGHT COMPLETE ONLY THE FOUNDATION BEFORE RUNNING OUT OF MONEY, AND THEN EVERYONE WOULD LAUGH AT YOU. THEY WOULD SAY, 'THERE'S THE PERSON WHO STARTED THAT BUILDING AND COULDN'T AFFORD TO FINISH IT!'*

If you want to be in ministry, you have to think like a professional. That means being interested in one's credit report, in fiduciary responsibility, and in creating systems for cash flow and income that will equate to the needed buying power to maintain a ministry. If you intend your ministry to grow to the point where you can get a loan or a mortgage, you need to be acutely interested in your debt-to-income ratio, which relates to how much money you have to pay out every month versus how much money you have coming in, and in your long-term economic and financial sustainability, which is your ability to make your ministry financially strong over a long period of time. Budgeting, establishing 501(c)(3) status, maintaining donors, and being honest and upfront about financial matters goes a long way to making sure your ministry can withstand the ups and downs of ministry long-term.

JOURNALING

- What excuses have you used to keep from giving to the Kingdom's work? How can you do better?
- What has been discussed in this chapter about ministry finances that you did not already know?
- What ministry do you partner with? Are you faithful in your partnership?

8 THE BEST THINGS IN LIFE ARE FREE

THIS entire book has been devoted to finances, giving, and examining financial states to help use the wisdom of the Scriptures to bring you to a better understanding of what God wants you to know about money. We all know the expression "money doesn't buy happiness," and in essence, we know that to be true. We also know that if we aren't in alignment with our finances, we can experience severe unhappiness in our lives. Not having our finances in order can make it so we experience the strains of debt, upset, and feeling like we are never going to catch up, which can increase our levels of stress and frustration, both immediately and long-term.

There are some things in life that do relate to money and giving that we should do freely and without cost, because they all relate to our attitude and character. No matter what we might be going through financially, we can always fall back on the wonder of these free things, given in abundance from God, our Father.

A CHEERFUL GIVER

Psalm 37:21: *THE WICKED BORROW AND NEVER REPAY, BUT THE GODLY ARE GENEROUS GIVERS.*

2 Corinthians 9:6-7: *REMEMBER THIS—A FARMER WHO PLANTS ONLY A FEW SEEDS WILL GET A SMALL CROP. BUT THE ONE WHO PLANTS GENEROUSLY WILL GET A GENEROUS CROP. YOU MUST EACH DECIDE IN YOUR HEART HOW MUCH TO GIVE. AND DON'T GIVE RELUCTANTLY OR IN RESPONSE TO PRESSURE. "FOR GOD LOVES A PERSON WHO GIVES CHEERFULLY."*

We often quote these verses when it's offering time, and it is very true that when it comes to giving financially, God does love a cheerful giver. We tend to only look at the characteristics of the giving in the context of the money, however, and we don't look at the relevance and importance of giving with a good heart or at having the true heart of a giver. While yes, it's important to look at what is being given, it is also very important to look at the heart of a giver.

Being willing to give reveals to us about where our hearts are. Where we are willing to give our money shows what's most important to us in our lives and where our values are. It also shows a level of unselfishness, one that is growing into the image of the Savior and less into the image of the flesh. It should be the goal of every one of us to develop the attributes of a cheerful giver, those that reflect an eagerness to do the right thing, to do right by others, and to give to others in order to see the work of God continue in all its various forms.

Giving is not just about money. It's also about giving of one's time, of one's talents, of one's abilities, of things that one might have that they no longer need, about giving gifts to people to encourage and edify them, and about being there for others. Giving of money is only the beginning of what God requires. When giving, a giver recognizes they aren't just giving something material, but something spiritual, to the person who receives what they have to offer. The more we embody these principles in our lives, the more we will see the world change.

FREELY RECEIVE AND FREELY GIVE

Matthew 10:5-15: *JESUS SENT OUT THE TWELVE APOSTLES WITH THESE INSTRUCTIONS: "DON'T GO TO THE GENTILES OR THE SAMARITANS, BUT ONLY TO THE PEOPLE OF ISRAEL—GOD'S LOST SHEEP. GO AND ANNOUNCE TO THEM THAT THE KINGDOM OF HEAVEN IS NEAR. HEAL THE SICK, RAISE THE DEAD, CURE THOSE WITH LEPROSY, AND CAST OUT DEMONS. GIVE AS FREELY AS YOU HAVE RECEIVED! "DON'T TAKE ANY MONEY IN YOUR MONEY BELTS—NO GOLD, SILVER, OR EVEN COPPER COINS. DON'T CARRY A TRAVELER'S BAG WITH A CHANGE OF CLOTHES AND SANDALS OR EVEN A WALKING STICK. DON'T HESITATE TO ACCEPT HOSPITALITY, BECAUSE THOSE WHO WORK DESERVE TO BE FED. "WHENEVER YOU ENTER A CITY OR VILLAGE, SEARCH FOR A WORTHY PERSON AND STAY IN HIS HOME UNTIL YOU*

LEAVE TOWN. WHEN YOU ENTER THE HOME, GIVE IT YOUR BLESSING. IF IT TURNS OUT TO BE A WORTHY HOME, LET YOUR BLESSING STAND; IF IT IS NOT, TAKE BACK THE BLESSING. IF ANY HOUSEHOLD OR TOWN REFUSES TO WELCOME YOU OR LISTEN TO YOUR MESSAGE, SHAKE ITS DUST FROM YOUR FEET AS YOU LEAVE. I TELL YOU THE TRUTH, THE WICKED CITIES OF SODOM AND GOMORRAH WILL BE BETTER OFF THAN SUCH A TOWN ON THE JUDGMENT DAY.

The idea of "freely giving" is often one people use to defend not giving to ministries or requiring a certain amount of money given in an offering (such as a tithe) to a church. They feel that the work of God should be given freely and without cost, and that ministries have no right to ask for money, based on the one verse of Matthew 10:8. As with all things Biblical, we need to have a greater understanding of the Scriptures than creating a hard and fast rule based on one passage of the Bible randomly applied out of context.

If we look carefully at the passage, Jesus was instructing the early apostles on their first mission and on the way they should conduct themselves. They were specifically told not to bring money with them, because they were worthy of the hospitality they should have received in each city. Jesus wasn't telling them just to give and not receive anything, but He was telling them that as they freely have received from those who provided for them, that they should too, freely give. It went in a synergy, of sorts; the early apostles received from God, they did what they were supposed to do, those they touched received from them, and they in turn freely gave back to the apostles in their keep and their provision.

Jesus was preparing the apostles for apostolic ministry after He ascended to heaven. For their work to flourish, it took the free giving of those who followed and their willingness to give in abundance of the gifts and graces that God bestowed upon each of them. It doesn't mean that they were supposed to give and never receive, however. Just as they were willing to give freely, so those who gave to them were supposed to be willing to give freely, too. If they were unwilling to host, or provide for them while they were there, then they were to shake the dust off their feet and go somewhere else where they would be received.

In ancient societies, they didn't have mega hotel chains or hostels for people to stay in when they were far from home. There weren't an abundance of restaurants to choose from when it was time to eat and you were out of town. People were, in accord with hospitality, to take in visitors and strangers as a sign that they were welcome. How hospitable a culture was to strangers said a lot about them as a people, and nations were judged on their hospitality (or lack thereof).

Today, we can't rely on people to take us in when we go to different regions or areas because we now have a different economic system that offers temporary lodging in the form of hotels and hostels worldwide. This means if we are to be able to freely give what God has given to us, we need to have the financial interest and backing of others. In this passage, Jesus was proving that the support needed in order to do the work of ministry has to come in more than just spiritual forms of prayer, good wishes, and encouraging words. To freely receive, people also must freely give to those who are providing spiritual approaches to everyday life and problems.

KEEP YOUR VOW

Ecclesiastes 5:1-7: *AS YOU ENTER THE HOUSE OF GOD, KEEP YOUR EARS OPEN AND YOUR MOUTH SHUT. IT IS EVIL TO MAKE MINDLESS OFFERINGS TO GOD. DON'T MAKE RASH PROMISES, AND DON'T BE HASTY IN BRINGING MATTERS BEFORE GOD. AFTER ALL, GOD IS IN HEAVEN, AND YOU ARE HERE ON EARTH. SO LET YOUR WORDS BE FEW. TOO MUCH ACTIVITY GIVES YOU RESTLESS DREAMS; TOO MANY WORDS MAKE YOU A FOOL. WHEN YOU MAKE A PROMISE TO GOD, DON'T DELAY IN FOLLOWING THROUGH, FOR GOD TAKES NO PLEASURE IN FOOLS. KEEP ALL THE PROMISES YOU MAKE TO HIM. IT IS BETTER TO SAY NOTHING THAN TO MAKE A PROMISE AND NOT KEEP IT. DON'T LET YOUR MOUTH MAKE YOU SIN. AND DON'T DEFEND YOURSELF BY TELLING THE TEMPLE MESSENGER THAT THE PROMISE YOU MADE WAS A MISTAKE. THAT WOULD MAKE GOD ANGRY, AND HE MIGHT WIPE OUT EVERYTHING YOU HAVE ACHIEVED. TALK IS CHEAP, LIKE DAYDREAMS AND OTHER USELESS ACTIVITIES. FEAR GOD INSTEAD.*

One of the biggest problems ministers face lies in those who commit to do things, especially give financially, and then do not follow through. Once I met a woman who insisted that she was supposed to give to the ministry. She gave once or twice, and then stopped giving. Even though at a later point in time she promised she would start again, she never did. I'd like to say this story is rare, but it's actually quite common. Many times people get caught up in the heat of the moment, the excitement about giving to something specific and being a part of something, and when the time goes on, they find that the promise they made to sow wasn't so easily maintained. When it gets inconvenient or isn't fun anymore, they stop giving all together.

If you have made a promise to give, to sow, or to do anything in particular for a ministry – then do it. Failing to keep vows means that ministers can't rely on steady income, and makes doing ministry that much harder. Beyond this, it proves that you aren't out of your flesh enough to assess the commitments you make and you are not a person of your word. Even though we don't talk seriously enough about being people who keep their word nowadays, it is just as important as it always has been. If we believe that words hold power, then the vows and promises we make must hold power, as well. To break that means that you have voided a spiritual power, akin to lying or using your words for deceitful purposes.

Making a vow is like making any other promise – be good to your word because to do anything else is to cause you to lie on yourself, and if you claim God told you to do it or moved you to do it, lie on God. God doesn't take that lightly. It's much easier to be a person of solid integrity.

GOOD JUDGMENT IN SOWING

Matthew 13:1-9: *LATER THAT SAME DAY JESUS LEFT THE HOUSE AND SAT BESIDE THE LAKE. A LARGE CROWD SOON GATHERED AROUND HIM, SO HE GOT INTO A BOAT. THEN HE SAT THERE AND TAUGHT AS THE PEOPLE STOOD ON THE SHORE. HE TOLD MANY STORIES IN THE FORM OF PARABLES, SUCH AS THIS ONE: "LISTEN! A FARMER WENT OUT TO PLANT SOME SEEDS. AS HE SCATTERED THEM ACROSS HIS FIELD, SOME SEEDS FELL ON A FOOTPATH, AND THE BIRDS CAME AND ATE THEM. OTHER SEEDS FELL ON SHALLOW SOIL WITH UNDERLYING ROCK. THE SEEDS SPROUTED QUICKLY BECAUSE THE SOIL WAS SHALLOW. BUT THE PLANTS SOON WILTED UNDER THE HOT SUN, AND SINCE THEY DIDN'T HAVE DEEP ROOTS, THEY DIED. OTHER SEEDS FELL AMONG THORNS THAT GREW UP AND CHOKED OUT THE TENDER PLANTS. STILL OTHER SEEDS FELL ON FERTILE SOIL, AND THEY PRODUCED A CROP THAT WAS THIRTY, SIXTY, AND EVEN A HUNDRED TIMES AS MUCH AS HAD BEEN PLANTED! ANYONE WITH EARS TO HEAR SHOULD LISTEN AND UNDERSTAND."*

Galatians 6:7: *DON'T BE MISLED—YOU CANNOT MOCK THE JUSTICE OF GOD. YOU WILL ALWAYS HARVEST WHAT YOU PLANT.*

There is no end to the number of people who claim to be in ministry and claim to be doing the work of the Kingdom...who clamor to tell you how much they need your money. In the past week, I have been hit up by no less than three different African ministers, asking for massive amounts of money (somewhere in the range of $30,000 to $300,000) and wanting to know how they can convince me to give them that money. I know nothing about them, they cannot verify anything of their work, and that means those will not be ministries where I will sow.

I don't mean to imply that we should give to everyone who comes along and asks us for money in the ministry. If we want to be people who see the harvest from what we sow, we need to be willing to give in good soil. When it comes to giving, there are a few guidelines on using good judgment in where – and when – to give:

- **First giving (tithes)** are to the ministry you attend or are directly connected to.

- **Second giving (offerings)** are to ministries endorsed by your leadership by being present at a service or guest preaching or ministries that you participate with, in some other way, secondarily from the primary ministry you are connected to.

- **Third giving (offerings)** are to ministries or good works that you know of firsthand.

Always beware giving to ministries that have absolutely no documentation or direct connection to a work that is 501(c)(3) or recognized as a charity in the nation where they are headquartered, that are solicit you without any foreknowledge of who they are or what they do, of ministries that are overseas and have no way to validate their work, or works that are otherwise shady in their nature.

THINGS WE SHOULDN'T BE "PAYING FOR" IN CHURCH

Micah 3:11: *YOU RULERS MAKE DECISIONS BASED ON BRIBES; YOU PRIESTS TEACH GOD'S LAWS ONLY FOR A PRICE; YOU PROPHETS WON'T PROPHESY UNLESS YOU ARE PAID. YET ALL OF YOU CLAIM TO DEPEND ON THE LORD. "NO HARM CAN COME TO US," YOU SAY, "FOR THE LORD IS HERE AMONG US."*

I meet a lot of people who swear by visiting a prophet, seeking a word, and paying them a large sum of money in return for the word they anticipate to receive. They feel the words they get from these individuals are legitimate, God-ordered, and purposed.

Does this sound familiar to anyone? It should. It is the same method and approach used by psychics, mediums, and witch doctors. The messages are either given from a script, are general enough to apply to any situation, or are developed by reading body language and hints given by those who come forward. The problem with the words that people receive from these sources are directly rooted in this vain system that people indulge in.

There is absolutely no reason why anyone, under any circumstances, should be paying to receive a "word" from someone in ministry leadership who claims to have a spiritual gift. This is also true for other forms of prophetic insight via gifts or formalized prophecy, including the function of dream interpretation, a word of wisdom or knowledge, or a word of encouragement. If a word is received for an individual, it should be given in obedience to God. There is nothing wrong with taking an offering or with giving a prophet or other leader an offering if that is the individual's desire to do so. In fact, I encourage people to bless those ministers who bless them with direct word and inspiration, and giving in response is something that should be done freely and without hesitation. There is something wrong, however, with giving word (or maybe we should say disguised word) for profit.

BEWARE THINGS THAT SOUND TOO GOOD TO BE TRUE

Proverbs 6:6-11: *TAKE A LESSON FROM THE ANTS, YOU LAZYBONES. LEARN FROM THEIR WAYS AND BECOME WISE! THOUGH THEY HAVE NO PRINCE OR GOVERNOR OR RULER TO MAKE THEM WORK, THEY LABOR HARD ALL SUMMER, GATHERING FOOD FOR THE WINTER. BUT YOU, LAZYBONES, HOW LONG WILL YOU SLEEP? WHEN WILL YOU WAKE UP? A LITTLE EXTRA SLEEP, A LITTLE MORE SLUMBER, A LITTLE FOLDING OF THE HANDS TO REST— THEN POVERTY WILL POUNCE ON YOU LIKE A BANDIT; SCARCITY WILL ATTACK YOU LIKE AN ARMED ROBBER.*

Proverbs 22:1: *CHOOSE A GOOD REPUTATION OVER GREAT RICHES; BEING HELD IN HIGH ESTEEM IS BETTER THAN SILVER OR GOLD.*

1 Thessalonians 5:22: *STAY AWAY FROM EVERY KIND OF EVIL.*

I am putting this in here as a final thought to this chapter because it isn't a topic that fit anywhere else in this book, but I felt it was of merit. Over the past six years, I have seen an increase in different business schemes that we used to classify as either "pyramid" or "Ponzi" schemes. While we used to treat such with caution, a rise in people who desire to be in ministry full-time without having to maintain secular employment has changed the attitude in such companies and made them newly desirable.

When it comes to independent representatives, contractors, or other businesses that operate by what's called a "multi-level marketing" model, it's not always easy to tell legitimate companies from scammers. There are legitimate MLM companies, and the way to tell the false from the true revolves around the complexity of the system and how involved one must go to recruit others just to maintain your position within the organization. Companies that operate a pyramid scheme structure are so-called because many individuals work and invest on the bottom levels in order to make money for those at the top, and there are very few individuals resting at the top place of profit.

I know and understand the temptations that we face in ministry, especially when the finances to do what we want to do are just not there. I also know what happens when we invest money in a project, especially a large amount of money, and how hard it can be to get out of something you have poured so much into. That means that just because something offers endless income potential and seems to be the answer to everything you seek doesn't mean it always is. We need to operate in a spirit of true discernment, good judgment, and investigation before we dive into anything that sounds like it is the answer to every prayer we have at that moment.

If you are interested in working in a sales company that allows you to do so independently, it is most prudent and wise to check into the company thoroughly before you make any commitments. Internet searches reveal those who are both happy and unhappy working with a company, and seeing both sides is important to decision-making. While a company is going to be all-too-eager to put their best foot forward to recruit new people to work for them, the sterling image a company may present is most likely one-sided and leaves out details. No matter how great a product might seem, if it is newer, it most likely hasn't been tested independently and there is no guarantee that others will be willing to try a new product. It's also wise to check out return policies, requirements for selling and working with the company, and general reputation of a company.

JOURNALING

- What kind of a giver are you? How can you work on being a cheerful giver?
- Why is it important to freely give if you have freely received?
- Why is keeping your word (vow) essential as a Christian?
- What have you "paid for" in church that you shouldn't have? What did you learn from that experience?
- Have you heard about any "too good to be true" programs out there that promise

incredible wealth? What was your response
to them?

9 FINANCIAL Q&A

Q: AS A CHRISTIAN, DOESN'T THE BIBLE TEACH THAT GOD WANTS ME TO BE POOR?

A: Let me say upfront that I don't think it's God's will that ANYONE be poor, living in poverty. I think the effects of poverty on mankind are directly related to the world in which we live, that is marred by sin and corruption. Poverty affects people in ways that relate to injustice, sorrow, unhappiness, and the feeling that they can't ever get ahead in their lives. These feelings aren't things that God would will upon someone, so I don't believe that poverty is something "willed" to us by God. The economics of this world are unjust, and I don't believe God has given some people money and caused others to deliberately live in lack.

Nonetheless, the concept that God wants us to be poor is perpetuated to this day in many

Christian circles. It has filtered down through the ages with the intent that people would give up their estates and possessions for the state churches, and do without themselves. The result were individuals who promoted the values of the church without compensation and without their own riches and financial aspirations to get in the way of other agendas.

Often used to defend this position is Matthew 19:16-30: *SOMEONE CAME TO JESUS WITH THIS QUESTION: "TEACHER, WHAT GOOD DEED MUST I DO TO HAVE ETERNAL LIFE?" "WHY ASK ME ABOUT WHAT IS GOOD?" JESUS REPLIED. "THERE IS ONLY ONE WHO IS GOOD. BUT TO ANSWER YOUR QUESTION—IF YOU WANT TO RECEIVE ETERNAL LIFE, KEEP THE COMMANDMENTS." "WHICH ONES?" THE MAN ASKED. AND JESUS REPLIED: "'YOU MUST NOT MURDER. YOU MUST NOT COMMIT ADULTERY. YOU MUST NOT STEAL. YOU MUST NOT TESTIFY FALSELY. HONOR YOUR FATHER AND MOTHER. LOVE YOUR NEIGHBOR AS YOURSELF.'" "I'VE OBEYED ALL THESE COMMANDMENTS," THE YOUNG MAN REPLIED. "WHAT ELSE MUST I DO?" JESUS TOLD HIM, "IF YOU WANT TO BE PERFECT, GO AND SELL ALL YOUR POSSESSIONS AND GIVE THE MONEY TO THE POOR, AND YOU WILL HAVE TREASURE IN HEAVEN. THEN COME, FOLLOW ME." BUT WHEN THE YOUNG MAN HEARD THIS, HE WENT AWAY SAD, FOR HE HAD MANY POSSESSIONS. THEN JESUS SAID TO HIS DISCIPLES, "I TELL YOU THE TRUTH, IT IS VERY HARD FOR A RICH PERSON TO ENTER THE KINGDOM OF HEAVEN. I'LL SAY IT AGAIN—IT IS EASIER FOR A CAMEL TO GO THROUGH THE EYE OF A NEEDLE THAN FOR A RICH PERSON TO ENTER THE KINGDOM OF GOD!" THE DISCIPLES WERE ASTOUNDED.*

"THEN WHO IN THE WORLD CAN BE SAVED?" THEY ASKED. JESUS LOOKED AT THEM INTENTLY AND SAID, "HUMANLY SPEAKING, IT IS IMPOSSIBLE. BUT WITH GOD EVERYTHING IS POSSIBLE." THEN PETER SAID TO HIM, "WE'VE GIVEN UP EVERYTHING TO FOLLOW YOU. WHAT WILL WE GET?" JESUS REPLIED, "I ASSURE YOU THAT WHEN THE WORLD IS MADE NEW AND THE SON OF MAN SITS UPON HIS GLORIOUS THRONE, YOU WHO HAVE BEEN MY FOLLOWERS WILL ALSO SIT ON TWELVE THRONES, JUDGING THE TWELVE TRIBES OF ISRAEL. AND EVERYONE WHO HAS GIVEN UP HOUSES OR BROTHERS OR SISTERS OR FATHER OR MOTHER OR CHILDREN OR PROPERTY, FOR MY SAKE, WILL RECEIVE A HUNDRED TIMES AS MUCH IN RETURN AND WILL INHERIT ETERNAL LIFE. BUT MANY WHO ARE THE GREATEST NOW WILL BE LEAST IMPORTANT THEN, AND THOSE WHO SEEM LEAST IMPORTANT NOW WILL BE THE GREATEST THEN."

There are many different issues raised in this passage, but I think the base issue addressed here is the question as to what makes one "good," more specifically, "good enough" in order to reap eternal life. It was, clearly, a question based in the law; in how to understand the law in order to live eternally and not face the question of peril or permanent death in the afterlife. The answers to the question reflect a student who felt he had it all under control, that he knew all and was prepared for all, and that based on his good works, he should have access to spiritual life. When Jesus told him to sell all he had and then follow Him, He wasn't saying this to the man so that one singular church could have a lot of money or to endorse a mention of poverty. Jesus told him to sell what he had and follow HIM, not live in a poverty state. The reason Jesus identified this issue to this man was clearly because he loved his possessions, and it was those possessions that was keeping him from finding eternal life. By trying to be "good enough," the young man was missing the point of true salvation.

The words of Jesus were not telling us that we can never have anything or that poverty is a necessity to be a Christian. Christ Himself clarifies that even though it might be hard for those with attachments to many things to enter the Kingdom, He said that with God, all things are possible, which means it is possible for a rich man to be saved. He was telling us that if we have a problem with our things interfering with our spiritual lives, we need to get rid of whatever is in the way. We assume the man wasn't going to receive anything else back by giving everything up, but we really don't know how the story would have ended had he been willing to part with what he had. Those whom God calls to give up something in their lives shall find what they seek, if they are only willing to give up what holds them back.

Q: IS IT WRONG FOR A CHRISTIAN TO HAVE SAVINGS?

A: Once again, the question as to whether or not we can have savings, a bank account, or set aside money for a specific purpose (such as retirement) is one that is based in misperceptions that we have of Scripture.

Luke 12:16-34: *THEN HE TOLD THEM A STORY: "A RICH MAN HAD A FERTILE FARM THAT PRODUCED FINE CROPS.*

[17] HE SAID TO HIMSELF, 'WHAT SHOULD I DO? I DON'T HAVE ROOM FOR ALL MY CROPS.' THEN HE SAID, 'I KNOW! I'LL TEAR DOWN MY BARNS AND BUILD BIGGER ONES. THEN I'LL HAVE ROOM ENOUGH TO STORE ALL MY WHEAT AND OTHER GOODS. AND I'LL SIT BACK AND SAY TO MYSELF, "MY FRIEND, YOU HAVE ENOUGH STORED AWAY FOR YEARS TO COME. NOW TAKE IT EASY! EAT, DRINK, AND BE MERRY!"' "BUT GOD SAID TO HIM, 'YOU FOOL! YOU WILL DIE THIS VERY NIGHT. THEN WHO WILL GET EVERYTHING YOU WORKED FOR?' "YES, A PERSON IS A FOOL TO STORE UP EARTHLY WEALTH BUT NOT HAVE A RICH RELATIONSHIP WITH GOD." THEN, TURNING TO HIS DISCIPLES, JESUS SAID, "THAT IS WHY I TELL YOU NOT TO WORRY ABOUT EVERYDAY LIFE—WHETHER YOU HAVE ENOUGH FOOD TO EAT OR ENOUGH CLOTHES TO WEAR. FOR LIFE IS MORE THAN FOOD, AND YOUR BODY MORE THAN CLOTHING. LOOK AT THE RAVENS. THEY DON'T PLANT OR HARVEST OR STORE FOOD IN BARNS, FOR GOD FEEDS THEM. AND YOU ARE FAR MORE VALUABLE TO HIM THAN ANY BIRDS! CAN ALL YOUR WORRIES ADD A SINGLE MOMENT TO YOUR LIFE? AND IF WORRY CAN'T ACCOMPLISH A LITTLE THING LIKE THAT, WHAT'S THE USE OF WORRYING OVER BIGGER THINGS? "LOOK AT THE LILIES AND HOW THEY GROW. THEY DON'T WORK OR MAKE THEIR CLOTHING, YET SOLOMON IN ALL HIS GLORY WAS NOT DRESSED AS BEAUTIFULLY AS THEY ARE. AND IF GOD CARES SO WONDERFULLY FOR FLOWERS THAT ARE HERE TODAY AND THROWN INTO THE FIRE TOMORROW, HE WILL CERTAINLY CARE FOR YOU. WHY DO YOU HAVE SO LITTLE FAITH? "AND DON'T BE CONCERNED ABOUT WHAT TO EAT AND WHAT TO DRINK. DON'T WORRY ABOUT SUCH THINGS. THESE THINGS DOMINATE THE THOUGHTS OF UNBELIEVERS ALL OVER THE WORLD, BUT YOUR FATHER ALREADY KNOWS YOUR NEEDS. SEEK THE

KINGDOM OF GOD ABOVE ALL ELSE, AND HE WILL GIVE YOU EVERYTHING YOU NEED. "SO DON'T BE AFRAID, LITTLE FLOCK. FOR IT GIVES YOUR FATHER GREAT HAPPINESS TO GIVE YOU THE KINGDOM. "SELL YOUR POSSESSIONS AND GIVE TO THOSE IN NEED. THIS WILL STORE UP TREASURE FOR YOU IN HEAVEN! AND THE PURSES OF HEAVEN NEVER GET OLD OR DEVELOP HOLES. YOUR TREASURE WILL BE SAFE; NO THIEF CAN STEAL IT AND NO MOTH CAN DESTROY IT. WHEREVER YOUR TREASURE IS, THERE THE DESIRES OF YOUR HEART WILL ALSO BE.

We already talked about the end of this passage, speaking on where our treasure is, there will our heart be, also. How we spend our money and what we save our money for tells a great deal about us as people and our priorities, thus making our finances a very tell-tale story about what is most important to us in our lives. I have heard people interpret this passage of Scripture, however, to indicate that we shouldn't ever save money, think about the future financially, or be fiscally responsible. To interpret this passage in this way is to misinterpret the purpose of what it is talking about. This passage is about trusting God to provide for our needs, and seeking Him as our primary source rather than seeking after the world for things. This doesn't mean we can't save money or have a bank account, but that we should seek Him for where we get our money and what we do with it.

Q: IS IT ALL RIGHT FOR A CHRISTIAN TO USE CREDIT CARDS?

A: That all depends on the Christian using them. I have found myself how useful the credit card can be, especially when travelling in ministry and travelling overseas. Often today hotels won't accept anything but credit cards and it is much easier to carry one or two cards than a thousand dollars in cash. They are a part of the economic system of our day, and they are, in many ways, much easier to handle than trying to figure out or carry cash. Used responsibly, there is nothing unchristian about using credit cards. It is not wise, however, to abuse them, and rack up excessive amounts of debt. So whether or not a Christian should use credit cards depends on the Christian and their ability to use credit responsibly. We should exercise wisdom and wise judgment when it comes to how we use credit.

Q: AS A CHRISTIAN, DO I HAVE TO PAY MY TAXES?

A: Yes.

Matthew 22:21: *RENDER THEREFORE THE THINGS THAT ARE CAESAR'S UNTO CAESAR; AND THE THINGS THAT ARE GOD'S UNTO GOD.* (KJV)

Paying taxes is a part of our Christian responsibility and witness. It doesn't mean we are in love with our government or all the decisions they make; in fact, the Christians of the first-century era often found their government leaders oppressive, immoral, and persecutory. Skipping out on paying taxes is against the precepts we claim to live by as Christians and is also lawlessness, which we know is antagonistic to what it means to be a Christian.

Q: SHOULD CHRISTIANS GAMBLE?

A: No.

Proverbs 13:11: *WEALTH FROM GET-RICH-QUICK SCHEMES QUICKLY DISAPPEARS; WEALTH FROM HARD WORK GROWS OVER TIME.*

Proverbs 16:33: *WE MAY THROW THE DICE, BUT THE LORD DETERMINES HOW THEY FALL.*

Ezekiel 7:19: *"THEY WILL THROW THEIR MONEY IN THE STREETS, TOSSING IT OUT LIKE WORTHLESS TRASH. THEIR SILVER AND GOLD WON'T SAVE THEM ON THAT DAY OF THE LORD'S ANGER. IT WILL NEITHER SATISFY NOR FEED THEM, FOR THEIR GREED CAN ONLY TRIP THEM UP."*

Luke 16:13: *"NO ONE CAN SERVE TWO MASTERS. FOR YOU WILL HATE ONE AND LOVE THE OTHER; YOU WILL BE DEVOTED TO ONE AND DESPISE THE OTHER. YOU CANNOT SERVE GOD AND BE ENSLAVED TO MONEY."*

Ephesians 4:28: *IF YOU ARE A THIEF, QUIT STEALING. INSTEAD, USE YOUR HANDS FOR GOOD HARD WORK, AND THEN GIVE GENEROUSLY TO OTHERS IN NEED.*

Truthfully nobody should gamble because life is enough of a risk and has enough complications without having to worry about job loss, making ends meet, and living within means without deliberately going out and wasting money with the high probability that you will lose it, and possibly more. It is irresponsible to spend time in casinos and other places that can quickly become addictive, and in playing games that are both immoral when gambling is involved, which too can become addictive. Don't waste what is God's and don't waste what rightfully belongs to your family.

Q: WHAT ABOUT GAMBLING ONLINE OR PLAYING "GAMBLING GAMES," SUCH AS POKER OR BINGO, WITHOUT BETTING?

A: Many do not realize that while there are no specific federal statues about internet gambling, there are some states that prohibit internet gambling, and internet gambling always runs a risk of landing someone in a bad spot. Even though it is being done online, it is still gambling and still wrong. If one is playing games without betting, then it is not gambling. There is nothing wrong with playing games for fun; but if at all possible, it can be good, especially when dealing with children, to find a game that does not have a gambling connotation.

Q: WHAT ABOUT LOTTERY TICKETS?

A: Lottery tickets are still a form of gambling and shouldn't be practiced by Christians. The odds of winning are extremely low and the tickets are simply a waste of money. Even though state lotteries do give some money to education, the majority of the money does indeed not go to a "worthy" cause.

Q: WHAT ABOUT THE STOCK MARKET?

A: I strongly advise individuals to pray about stock market trades, especially given I have met people who experienced severe losses in the market based on things considered "sure bets." There are many who believe in investing, and doing so, wisely, and there is nothing wrong with maintaining a proper perspective when it comes to investments. It is my personal opinion that stock market investments can take on a nature of white collar gambling, but this is my opinion, and not something I require people to accept as Gospel or feel the same way about as I do. Whether or not to deal in stocks is a personal choice, and something that may be done within certain guidelines in a company or a business that one works for. Although stockbrokers and advisers may be in positions where they seem knowledgeable, they aren't psychics and can't predict a sudden crash or stock market falter; all they do is read obvious signs, with many of them being paid on commission incentives and faltering when a client removes their investments from the company. When dealing in stocks, move in wisdom, move in information, and educate yourself as much as possible in the process and the risks as well as the rewards.

Q: SHOULD I CO-SIGN A MORTGAGE, LOAN, OR CREDIT CARD APPLICATION WITH A PERSON I LIVE WITH, BUT AM

NOT MARRIED TO?

A: It is considered financially inadvisable to enter into a long-term financial agreement with someone that you are not bound to by a legal, committed relationship. Yes, it might seem like a good idea at the time, as a way to save money or to get something that seems to solidify a relationship in the right direction, but the court system is flooded with agreements gone sour due to relationships that weren't legal and didn't make things work long-term. Being in a relationship with no legal standing means it's just that – a relationship with no legal standing – and makes figuring out what belongs to who and who owes for what that much more complicated if the relationship doesn't work. Hold off on major joint financial decisions until after you are married.

Q: IS IT IMMORAL FOR CHRISTIANS TO DECLARE BANKRUPTCY?

A: It all depends upon the reason for the bankruptcy. The number one cause of bankruptcy is medical debt, which can be incurred for a variety of reasons. This means not all bankruptcies come about because of a circumstance that is within someone's feasible control, and sometimes having to start all over again becomes a viable question. Bankruptcy has a lot of negatives aside from the moral aspect, including the fact that bankruptcy all but destroys one's credit. Although it's not impossible to build it back up again, the fact that one has a bankruptcy always remains on their credit record. Bankruptcies can cause you to be denied credit in your life even long after you've finished the process. When would a bankruptcy be acceptable? Sometimes we "inherit" debt from a deceased relative or friend. In this instance, and especially if you can't afford to cover it, a bankruptcy is not immoral. It is also not immoral if the debt you have acquired is due to a circumstance you can't control, such as handling an estate, medical circumstances, or providing care for a loved one. Debt becomes immoral when you had control over the debt you acquired, such as misuse of credit cards or over-spending.

Q: HOW OLD SHOULD MY CHILDREN BE BEFORE I START TEACHING THEM ABOUT THE PRECEPTS OF GIVING?

A: Awhile back I saw a show on television featuring a Christian family that took a tithe out of their children's weekly allowance for offering – and truth be told, many of these children were under ten! Children are never too young to learn the basics of giving and its importance. We learn to be givers, it's not something born in us. Very young children can be taught sharing and concern for others. Including your children in goodwill donations to charity is important, by having them select some of their own old toys or clothes to give away. When schools do food drives, let your children pick out some canned goods to donate and have them bring them in themselves. Once they are working either through a home allowance and/or a job, having their own money, they should know the importance of tithing and be prepared to give their tithe. The best thing you can do is incorporate giving into their lifestyle by having it be the family lifestyle. They learn best by doing, and if it is a family precept, they indeed will give.

Q: WEREN'T TITHES ONLY GATHERED FROM CROPS? WHAT DEFENSE IS THERE FOR TAKING A TITHE IN THE FORM OF MONEY?

A: The past few years I have seen arguments like this one pop up on internet forums and social media networks. It wasn't an argument I had ever heard prior, and I have to admit that I haven't heard it invoked all that much. If you do a search on the question, many different websites come up with different information and different opinions.

When it comes to tithing, we need to realize that the Bible was written in an agricultural society, and crops were used as barter for exchanges and payments. This means that crops were used as a monetary source, and bringing a tithe of crops equated to bringing an equated value of money. This is why the first line of tithes always related to crops: because they were considered a part of the financial bartering and economic systems present in Biblical times.

There were options, however, for tithing that did relate to money.

Deuteronomy 14:22-29: *"YOU MUST SET ASIDE A TITHE OF YOUR CROPS—ONE-TENTH OF ALL THE CROPS YOU HARVEST EACH YEAR. BRING THIS TITHE TO THE DESIGNATED PLACE OF WORSHIP—THE PLACE THE LORD YOUR GOD CHOOSES FOR HIS NAME TO BE HONORED—*

AND EAT IT THERE IN HIS PRESENCE. THIS APPLIES TO YOUR TITHES OF GRAIN, NEW WINE, OLIVE OIL, AND THE FIRSTBORN MALES OF YOUR FLOCKS AND HERDS. DOING THIS WILL TEACH YOU ALWAYS TO FEAR THE LORD YOUR GOD. "NOW WHEN THE LORD YOUR GOD BLESSES YOU WITH A GOOD HARVEST, THE PLACE OF WORSHIP HE CHOOSES FOR HIS NAME TO BE HONORED MIGHT BE TOO FAR FOR YOU TO BRING THE TITHE. IF SO, YOU MAY SELL THE TITHE PORTION OF YOUR CROPS AND HERDS, PUT THE MONEY IN A POUCH, AND GO TO THE PLACE THE LORD YOUR GOD HAS CHOSEN. WHEN YOU ARRIVE, YOU MAY USE THE MONEY TO BUY ANY KIND OF FOOD YOU WANT—CATTLE, SHEEP, GOATS, WINE, OR OTHER ALCOHOLIC DRINK. THEN FEAST THERE IN THE PRESENCE OF THE LORD YOUR GOD AND CELEBRATE WITH YOUR HOUSEHOLD. AND DO NOT NEGLECT THE LEVITES IN YOUR TOWN, FOR THEY WILL RECEIVE NO ALLOTMENT OF LAND AMONG YOU. "AT THE END OF EVERY THIRD YEAR, BRING THE ENTIRE TITHE OF THAT YEAR'S HARVEST AND STORE IT IN THE NEAREST TOWN. GIVE IT TO THE LEVITES, WHO WILL RECEIVE NO ALLOTMENT OF LAND AMONG YOU, AS WELL AS TO THE FOREIGNERS LIVING AMONG YOU, THE ORPHANS, AND THE WIDOWS IN YOUR TOWNS, SO THEY CAN EAT AND BE SATISFIED. THEN THE LORD YOUR GOD WILL BLESS YOU IN ALL YOUR WORK."

In other words, if a tithe couldn't be presented in person, the individual had to go to a place that God would choose, convert the tithe for silver, into a monetary form, to make sure that the sacrifice of such was completed and brought to the Levites in each place.

Leviticus 27:30-33: *"ONE-TENTH OF THE PRODUCE OF*

THE LAND, WHETHER GRAIN FROM THE FIELDS OR FRUIT FROM THE TREES, BELONGS TO THE LORD AND MUST BE SET APART TO HIM AS HOLY. IF YOU WANT TO BUY BACK THE LORD'S TENTH OF THE GRAIN OR FRUIT, YOU MUST PAY ITS VALUE, PLUS 20 PERCENT. COUNT OFF EVERY TENTH ANIMAL FROM YOUR HERDS AND FLOCKS AND SET THEM APART FOR THE LORD AS HOLY. YOU MAY NOT PICK AND CHOOSE BETWEEN GOOD AND BAD ANIMALS, AND YOU MAY NOT SUBSTITUTE ONE FOR ANOTHER. BUT IF YOU DO EXCHANGE ONE ANIMAL FOR ANOTHER, THEN BOTH THE ORIGINAL ANIMAL AND ITS SUBSTITUTE WILL BE CONSIDERED HOLY AND CANNOT BE BOUGHT BACK."

If a tithe was exchanged for money, there was an additional tax on the fifth of the value of that tithe that also had to be paid. The reason for this – if there was a direct income generated on the item instead of giving the item itself – there was a higher profit value that thus had to be offered to the Kingdom.

This means that not all tithes were given in the form of crops, and that money was used at times in keeping with the circumstances found in ancient Israel. Being most of us do not live in an agrarian society that is dependent on crops, nor that crops are used for currency, we give our tithe in the form of money today, because it is how we are compensated and paid in our current economy.

Q: MY SPOUSE IS NOT A BELIEVER AND WILL NOT TITHE OR GIVE. WHAT CAN I DO?

A: With most couples working separate jobs, it often means households have two sources of income. If you have your own income source, tithe from your own money. If you do not have your own separate income source but receive an allowance of sorts, tithe from that. It doesn't matter that it isn't a million dollars. What matters is in your heart, and that you desire to do what God has asked of you!

Q: I DON'T FEEL LIKE I HAVE EXTRA MONEY TO TITHE, AND THEREFORE I FEEL LIKE I SHOULD BE EXEMPT. AM I?

A: I am sure that Jesus didn't particularly feel like going to the cross, but He did it anyway. I am sure that Moses got tired of going before Pharaoh, but he did it anyway. I am sure that Ruth got tired of gleaning in the fields, but she did it anyway. I am also sure that there is somebody in the world with far less money than you who is making the effort to tithe. Tithing isn't done out of "extra money" but is rather the first-fruits of your offering to God. It is the first ten percent, not the ten percent that is left over after you've covered all your expenses and done whatever you want with your money. Tithing must be a priority because God is a priority and He is first in your life. Telling God you can't give Him His ten percent is telling Him that He is not first in your life. If you set the tithe first, you will always be able to afford it and will not need to convince yourself that you need an exemption! You don't have to tithe, because God will not force you, but you will not receive the blessing for tithing if you refuse to do it.

Q: HOW MUCH MONEY SHOULD I AIM TO GIVE IN OFFERINGS EACH MONTH?

A: Since offerings are not a regulated form of giving unless it is in the form of a commitment to a ministry partnership (which is then an amount that you commit to give), it depends upon the month and what you are giving to. Let God guide you as to how much you should give beyond your tithe for offerings each month.

Q: AM I WITHIN MY LEGAL RIGHTS TO SEEK OUT RESTITUTION IF I HAVE BEEN WRONGED FINANCIALLY?

A: Although I would advise you to seek out other alternatives aside from court action because the system has this way of being notoriously unfair and making situations that seem to be real obvious and real simple not so simple or obvious, if another way is impossible, you are within your legal rights to seek out restitution if you have been wronged as long as you are not doing so out of a spirit of vengefulness but seek a genuine righting of the situation. From a spiritual perspective, I believe that we should attempt to resolve our differences ourselves as often as it is possible, and we should also employ a spirit of love and forgiveness before we start pursuing things in legal battles that cost us more money and more time. It's all about motives.

Q: WHEN I GET AN INCREASE IN PAY, SHOULD MY TITHES AND OFFERINGS INCREASE?

A: Yes. Since the tithe is ten percent of your total income, if you have received an increase in your income total your tithe does too increase. If you have more money coming into your life, it should allow for you to be more generous and giving in all other areas of your life, including offerings.

Q: IS THE FIGURE WE CALCULATE FOR A TITHE OUR INCOME BEFORE OR AFTER TAXES?

A: Before, as a tithe is ten percent of your total income, not just what you take home after you are paid. Remember, a tithe is technically an ancient form of taxation, thus it would have been calculated before any other dues, taxes, or other things were paid from one's income.

On a side note: many Christians debate about tithing on an income tax return. If your income tax return is returned to you and you based your tithe on your income prior to taxation, then you have already paid your tithe on that money. If you receive a return that is over the amount you paid into the system due to benefits and credits, then you need to pay tithes on that difference. For example: if you are getting a child credit that is thousands of dollars, then that is an income benefit and you should pay tithes on that money. Income is income, no matter how it comes to you.

Q: DOES PURCHASING BOOKS OR ALBUM SERIES FROM A MINISTRY COUNT AS GIVING?

A: Although such a purchase does benefit a ministry because you are buying products offered to help you grow and develop spiritually, it isn't the same as giving a free-will offering, gift, or tithe because you are buying a specific product with a specific return to you in mind. If you are purchasing the item or items to give to someone else, that will count as giving!

Q: I HAVE A FRIEND WHO I KNOW IS IN FINANCIAL TROUBLE BUT I DON'T WANT TO EMBARRASS HER BY OFFERING HER MONEY. SHOULD I WAIT UNTIL SHE ASKS ME FOR MONEY? OR IS THERE SOMETHING I CAN DO IN THE MEANTIME?

A: I am very touched by your desire to give and that shows a great heart and a giving spirit. You are correct that offering your friend money might embarrass her and I would wait and see if she comes to you. In the meantime, there are ways you can give to her that will help her out without embarrassing her. When you go shopping, pick up a little something extra for your friend and give it to her either as it is or cook a meal and bring it over to her. Listen to her speak of things she needs, and if you can afford it, purchase it for her. You can always offer her a helping hand or offer to listen to talk if she needs something. You could buy her a special present, something that she's needed or wanted for a while. If she's out of work, volunteer to help her look over her resume for suggestions or to help her in her job search, maybe even baby-sitting for her. Encourage her that even though things are tough for her right now, God cares about her and so do you and other people in her life. In other words, don't stop being her friend because she is in a financial bind. Keep being her friend and be there for her.

Q: IS IT ACCEPTABLE FOR CHRISTIANS TO LIVE ON GOVERNMENT PROGRAMS?

A: The more I hear about this issue, the more disagreement I discover as pertains to it. Many conservative ministers debate the issue from a laziness perspective, assuming anyone who uses government-subsidized programs to be lazy or unmotivated. While I am sure there are some who are on government assistance who are lazy, it's not possible to say that's how everyone is or how everyone feels about it, and it minimizes the fact that there are people who are in genuine need and who are eligible for such programs. There are many people who are seriously disabled and unable to work, who have worked to "pay the man" for years and now the "man" is not paying them back. here are many who can't make ends meet, even with working. Some people lose their jobs, through no fault of their own, and can't find another job because there aren't any new jobs. Unemployment only pays half of the paycheck and is often demanding and unreasonable and will cease benefits if they feel one is not adequately searching for employment. Without family or a support system to fall back on, sometimes there aren't any other alternatives or answers.

For this, I blame modern-day Christians who have replaced God's principles of caring for those less fortunate with a give me, give me, give me attitude rooted in unblessed selfishness. If we want a world where people don't have to rely on government subsidies, then that means the church needs to get in a giving place and stand active on the front lines of supporting its own.

As for the moral issue of using government programs, we need to separate the notions of use from misuse. Clearly misusing and abusing government programs is wrong, just as it is wrong to misuse any program. As for using them, these programs are funded by our tax dollars. If we are paying taxes or have paid taxes, then we are paying for our use of programs and in a country where we pay out-of-pocket for medical, educational, dental, and child care where other countries in a similar tax bracket do not, there is nothing immoral about having to use government programs for a time to help one get back on their feet if one is eligible.

The one thing we need to be cautious about is the secret side-effects many of these programs have that they don't readily tell you about. For example, if you need emergency heating assistance in some states, they will seize any existing funds in your bank account. Food stamp programs also sometimes seize any excess funds, including college and retirement accounts. Welfare programs often expect you to, once having a job as part of the "welfare to work" program, pay back any and all funds given to you while on welfare by seizing your paychecks in full. It is very important that, if alternatives exist, one finds them because the consequences of using money that, even though is technically ours, the government is in possession of, can be so severe that it lands one in greater trouble than when they started.

JOURNALING

- What questions do you have about finances? Write them here and then research the answers.

ABOUT THE AUTHOR
DR. LEE ANN B. MARINO,
PH.D., D.MIN., D.D.

Dr. Lee Ann B. Marino, Ph.D., D.Min., D.D.
(she/her) is "everyone's favorite theologian" leading Gen X, Millennials, and Gen Z with expertise in leadership training, queer and feminist theology, general religion, and apostolic theology. A graduate of Apostolic Preachers College, Dr. Marino has served in ministry since 1998 and was ordained as a pastor in 2002 and an apostle in 2010. She founded what is now Spitfire Apostolic Ministries in 2004. Under her ministry heading Dr. Marino is founder and overseer of Sanctuary International Fellowship Tabernacle – SIFT (the original home of National Coming Out Sunday) and Chancellor of Apostolic University.

Affectionately nicknamed "the Spitfire," Dr. Marino has spent over two decades as an "apostle, preacher, and teacher" (2 Timothy 1:11), exercising her personal mandate to become "all things to all people" (1 Corinthians 9:22). Her embrace of spiritual issues (both technical and intimate) has found its home among both seekers and believers, those who desire spiritual answers to today's issues.

Dr. Marino has preached throughout the United States, Puerto Rico, and Europe in hundreds of religious services and experiences throughout the years. A history maker in her own right, she has spent over two decades in advocacy, education, and work for and within minority spiritual communities (including African American, Hispanic, and LGBTQ+). She has also served as the first woman on all-male synods, councils, and panels, as well as the first preacher or speaker welcomed of a different race, sexual orientation, or identity among diverse communities. Today, Dr. Marino's work extends to over one hundred countries as she hosts the popular *Kingdom Now* podcast, which is in the top twenty percentile of all podcasts worldwide. She is also the author of over thirty books and the popular Patheos column, *Leadership on Fire*. To date, she has had four bestselling titles within their subject matter: *Understanding Demonology, Spiritual Warfare, Healing, and Deliverance: A Manual for the Christian Minister; Ministry School Boot Camp: Training for Helps Ministries, Appointments, and Beyond; Surrounded By So Great a Cloud of Witnesses: Women of Faith Who Revolutionized History;* and *Ministering to LGBTQs – and Those Who Love Them.*

As a public icon and social media influencer, Dr. Marino advocates for healthy body image (curvy/full-figured), queer representation (as a demisexual/aromantic), and albinism awareness, as a model. Known to those she works with, she is spiritual mom, teacher, leader, professor, confidant, and friend. She continues to transform, receiving new teaching, revelation, and insight in this thing we call "ministry." Through years of spiritual growth and maturity, Dr. Marino stands as herself, here to present what God has given to her for any who have an ear to hear.

For more information, visit her website at kingdompowernow.org.

www.ingramcontent.com/pod-product-compliance
Lightning Source LLC
Chambersburg PA
CBHW061822040426
42447CB00012B/2772